Body
and
Soul

Foreword

Any poet will tell you that being a poet isn't just a state of mind. All true poets live and breathe the passion and pain of their art - to the very fibre of their being.

Poetry gives them wings to soar above the mundane and trivial. In any true poet the spirit of poetry burns bright and fierce.

And when poets write, they write with their whole body and soul. Nothing is held back.

All the great poets have been able to strip away the concerns and fears that can put a barrier in their way. They write from the heart and express themselves in a manner which reveals their inner selves.

In this compilation we have endeavoured to bring together the work of a group of poets who all have that one strength in common. They write poetry because they have a deep, powerful urge to describe their emotions - to set them down in words. They want to both reveal and explore themselves through the written word. There is no art more demanding or difficult. You, the reader, can be the judge of their success.

But there is no doubt that when poets put their *Body and Soul* into their work, the results can be dramatic.

Peter Quinn, Editor

Contents

The poets who have contributed to this volume are listed below, along with the relevant page upon which their work can be found.

65	Neil Simms	93	Michael Buckley
66	Chantelle Walker	94	Daniel Francis
67	Alan Green	95	Gabrielle Cannon
68	David Faggiani	96	Muriel Clark
	David Lobodzinski		Heather Ferrier
69	Albert Leonard	97	Joan M Jones
	Sabiné Ridge		Emma Wilkinson
70	Elsie Hamilton	98	Connie Watson
71	Beverly Beaumont	99	Sarah Tucker
72	Graham Scotson	100	June Hellewell
	Daniella McLenaghan		Emily Beswick
73	David Grant	101	Geoff Wilson
	Lisa Smith		Mary Magilton
74	Joan Dawson	102	Tina Tamsho-Thomas
75	Rosemary Hawes	103	Lilac Milton
76	Kelly Horsfall	104	David Glover
	Jenni Edward		Jean Wood
77	Kathryn Russell	105	Lynne Goddard
	Pat McAleese		Thomas McGrath
78	Catherine Coward	106	Nikki Day
79	Janet Garner	107	Margaret Ridgway
80	Christine Skeer		Sylvia Lee-Wild
	Frances Rochelle	108	John Holmes
	Barrie	109	Tom Gorton
81	Jessica Street	110	Ann Blair
	Chris Smith	111	Barbara Murray
82	Anthony Bardsley		Maureen Holt
83	Michael Bergin	112	Don McLean
84	Lesley Allsopp	113	Antony Haselton
	Michael Skeffington	114	Ruth Goldsworthy
85	Ian Jenkins	115	S L P-Adams
	Janice Brierley		D Doyle
86	Rosemary Chesters	116	Francis Hogan
87	Leanne McGing	117	Isobel Cullen
88	Jackie Connelly	118	Brian Williams
	Ken Bradbury Harrop	119	Heather McCavish
89	Jo Rainford		Lauren Gould
	Debbie Seddon	120	Jean Beasor
90	Sarah Jane Price	121	Emily Ablett
91	Malcolm F Young	122	Georgina Southern
92	Eric Taylor	123	K Moyses
	Anantha Rudravajhala	124	Rachel Cromwell
93	Andrew Henderson		Elizabeth Gill

125	Vera Tague	160	David Bridgewater
126	Christine Hale	161	Michael Kenneth
127	Heather Cattle		Barnes
128	H Kenny		Anna Torpey
	Andy Powell	162	Joan Flynn
129	Tony Tasak		Louise Forshaw
130	Joyce Loftus	163	Tommy McBride
131	Janet Hughes	164	Matthew James Arnold
132	Viki Duffy	165	Jennifer Donald
	Shirley Tomlinson	166	Gareth Rogers
133	Harry Shaw		June Rose-Hobson
134	P McDowell	167	Frankie Shepherd
135	Mary Barnes		Kayleigh Hogg
136	Charlotte Hughes	168	Carol Haigh
	Kathrine Taylor	169	Anthony Morrin
137	Elsie Prenton		M Sargent
138	Paula Morris	170	Angela Overend
139	Nick Buchanan	171	Barbara Langton
140	William Carr		Rose Henry
	Lydia Bowdidge	172	Sarah Leahey
141	Barbara Nuttall		Jessica McClurg
142	Sue Farley	173	Margaret Lyon
143	James A Sambrooks	174	Julie Borkwood
144	Sarah Louise Carroll		L M Boyd
145	Sybil Willcox	175	Joey Langton
	Lauren Brooks	176	Mary Angela Miller
146	Robert Warwick Green		Robert Evans
147	Shaun Daly	177	Lynda Day Bidston
148	D F Jones	178	Albert E J Carpenter
149	John Mutton		Rachael Ross
	Amanda Dodd	179	Matthew Paul De-Gier
150	Stephen Thelwell	180	Rebecca Jackson
151	Mary Murray		Gill Hulse
152	M T Daly	181	Brenda Clarke
153	Jean Beattie	182	Suzanne Flynn
	Ans Dodd Prins	183	Jo Goddard
154	Polly Pawson	184	Ray Owens
155	J I Sherlock		John Dixon
156	Jean Broadley	185	Julian Warwick
157	Dave Harley		Rod Trott
	Ken Horton	186	Zita Abila
158	Patricia McDonough		Mark Hogan
159	Kathleen Furlong	187	Beryl Leece

187	David Favager	214	Arthur Bradbury
188	Christine Rowley	215	D Parry
	Janet Jones		Jean Shingler
189	Reginald Waywell	216	Daniel Cheung
	Sophie Kavanagh		Larissa Weston
190	Diane Burrows	217	Kelly Hellon
191	Vicki Wroe	218	Marjorie Lomax
192	Gloria Hamlett		Dawn L Edwards
	Victoria Webb	219	Cathy Dwyer
193	Darren Anthony	220	Ian Hughes
	Stoker		P J Chadwick
194	Nicky Lewis	221	J Rapilliard
	Norma Edwards		Bill Huddleston
195	Anna Sabti	222	Derek Culley
196	Andrew Rawlings		David Brown
	Paige Dady	223	Brian Sadler
197	L Chisnall		
198	Hayley Jones		
	Felicia Rochelle Isaacs		
199	Louise Butler		
200	Andrea King		
	Barbara Jardine		
201	Naheed Nadeem		
202	Yvette Parker		
	Jean Hopwood		
203	Doris Thomson		
204	Robert Burgess		
205	Miriam Duddridge		
206	Sarah Louise Smith		
	Pauline Ann Green		
207	Richard Dunne		
208	Norma Wilson		
	Lesley Michell		
209	Albert E Bird		
	Doreen M Evans		
210	Anthony Atkinson		
	Yvonne St Clair		
211	Paul Yates		
	Colin McCombe		
212	Jennie Bullock		
	Marilynne Harrison		
213	Harry Boyle		
214	Pam Lewis		

FIRST AND LAST VOYAGE

A maiden voyage from Liverpool
Some say the greatest of all
But as she neared the waters of icy cool
Her journey was about to stall
Meanwhile, in frozen waters
An iceberg was drifting on course
Titanic, laden with sons and daughters
Would meet its incredible force
On this dark and cold night
Passengers would all sing and dine
Not knowing when out went the lights
It was the end of the Titanic and the White Star Line
Then between the mist and sea
Appeared the shadowy figure of doom
Bells are ringing and sailors flee
There's ice in the engine room
As lifeboats are lowered and events unfold
The captain retreats to a watery end
This story will be told and told
Please God, save our souls, send, send, send

Joshua Brian De Vere, Frodsham, Cheshire

Born in Warrington, **Joshua Brian De Vere** has interests including playing the guitar, writing songs and playing golf. "My work is influenced by John Lennon and Spike Milligan, and I would describe my style as poetic storytelling." Aged 56, Joshua is a property developer with an ambition to write a bestselling thriller. "My biggest fantasy is to blast off in a space shuttle and my worst nightmare is an air crash at night in the sea. The person I would most like to meet is Kofi Annan because he is an honest person with a great understanding of global communications," added Joshua.

MADNESS

What goes around comes around,
In a vortex of what was and is and is to come,
In destiny is somehow bound,
To intertwine then come undone.

The helix unending,
All you know is all that you can see,
Knowledge is an image pending,
Truth that soon could set you free.

Just wait your turn,
In the end you'll know but all too late,
Many things you cannot learn,
Exhaust your time searching your fate.

If ignorance is truth,
Then only lies can lie ahead of you,
Too hard for you to comprehend,
Until the very end.

Christopher Johnson, Anderton, Cheshire

SCOTLAND

A holiday home to appreciate this God made land,
Wildlife and it's dwelling showing his plan.
For beauty that will last for many years after,
The swallows have left their residencies in the barn rafters.

The lake, it is framed between two mountain points,
Habitats joined with many seamless joints.
A seagull stands sentry on a lone rock,
A pair of ducks disturb, the glassy still loch.

On a hill not far away, what a magnificent sight,
A different perspective, from a great height.
An experience for both, the body and the soul,
See all that surround you as upwards you stroll.

The variety of landscapes in such a small space,
Give us an insight into God's power and wonder and grace.
So then, let us be thankful in the way that we live,
Looking after the world that for all God did give.

Jonathan Pike, Northwich, Cheshire

IT'S A CAT'S LIFE

Starving,
You feed me.
Sleeping,
You leave me.
Playing,
You tease me.
Hiding,
You find me.
Purring,
You stroke me.
Hurting,
You hold me.
Living,
Here is cat heaven.

Angela Pritchard, Sandbach, Cheshire

A STARTER FOR YOU

If I were a strawberry
Small and sweet
I'd beg you to pick me
And eat
My soft tender body
My red flowing juice
Handle me nicely
Then seduce
Savour my flavour
Then savour my taste
But don't dribble any
As that's just a waste

Toni Prosser, Wallasey, Cheshire

Dedicated to Davey for lighting the way to Dandyland

14

ODE TO MY BEST MATE

Here lies the body of Peter Carr
He owned a JCB and a motor car
The jobs he did were always sound
But now he is six feet underground
No-one knows why he did fail
Perhaps it was the home brewed ale
Or maybe his early decline
Was due to his homemade rhubarb wine
Alas, the stuff took its toll
And now he's down a six foot hole
Undeterred, he rose again
A game of snooker was his aim
Just as we thought he'd gone to heaven
He came back with a one-four-seven

John Harrison, Widnes, Cheshire

TIME OUT

Close your eyes and drift away
Think back to days of yesteryear
Wrap yourself up in lovely dreams
Lanes to ramble between green fields
Forests of trees with multicoloured leaves
Carpets of bluebells, wild flowers that please
Smells so delightful in the morning breeze

Stop, pause and listen to nature's sounds
Babbling brooks in which frogs abound
Scuttling creatures low on the ground
Trilling of birds, so many around
The buzzing of bees, squirrels in trees
Be glad to enjoy all these wonderful scenes

Celia Cholmondeley, Warrington, Cheshire

TSUNAMI

The knowledge man holds is immense
But the power of nature transcends
In seconds, destruction descends
And we struggle to make any sense

A power that has shown no remorse
That makes us tremble and cry
We search for the reason why
But there is none, it's nature of course

Bill Batcock, Warrington, Cheshire

Born in Golborne, **Bill Batcock** has interests including walking, reading and keeping fit. "I started writing poetry many years ago and my work is influenced by the ever-changing world," he explained. "I would like to be remembered as a nice guy and my ambition is for a long and happy life. I am a 56-year-old director, and the person I would most like to meet is the explorer Ernest Shackleton who was an inspiration to everyone." Bill is married to Christine and they have children Russell and Helen.

BETTER

Love means space and time to grow,
And in our hearts each seed we sow.
With this love we prove that we,
Can a better person be.

So whilst our children we do hold,
We also teach them to be bold.
To take the first step on the way,
To goodness each and every day.

And so my son the years have gone.
I hope you think that I'm the one,
That gave you love and made you free,
To a better person be.

As the years are creeping past,
I hope the lessons learned will last,
To pass onto your children too,
For better people just like you.

Frances Furnace, Ellesmere Port, Cheshire

RECKLESS WORDS

Words ricochet around the room,
With spear like splinters to pierce the heart.
Glinting, they transcend the gloom,
From barbed tongue to tear apart.

Proudly they demean, degrade,
Peeling away all dignity.
Psyche, constrained, begins to fade,
Revealing base humanity.

When they have spurted from the fount,
Cascading o'er the withering form,
With acid smouldering in the wound,
They leave a body wasted, worn.

Disguised in sudden laughter,
Sailing on a smile,
Retreating from the slaughter,
They pause and rest awhile.

Helen Broady, Runcorn, Cheshire

ODE TO ATHENS

Bombs galore, what's next in store
No doubt there will be many more
Athletes with anxious faces
Bravely running through their paces
Thinking
Olympic medals, what are they worth
If we're all dead in the earth
Security has let us down
We need more forces on the ground
Why should we keep on competing
When our deaths we could be meeting
Will we attain olympic gold
Or watch Greek tragedy unfold?

Gillian Morrissey, Dukinfield, Cheshire

WHOSE BRITAIN?

The rolling hills, the squalid city slums
The rich in greed and splendour
The poor in health and spirit
Whose Britain?

The religion of must-have materialism
A culture of gambling for riches untold
Whose Britain?

Have today, have on credit, pay tomorrow
Never mind the debt, never mind the future of repayment
Whose Britain?

Rethink, respond, renew

Brian Platt, Marple, Cheshire

SNOW

Snow falls from the trees
Daggers hang from the eaves
Snow lies there glistening
A thick blanket of snow
Cold snow undisturbed
In the winter freeze
Crude fingers frost bitten
Poke tentatively through
The blanket of the white desert
Cars like choc ices waiting
To be unwrapped
Now the doors start to open
And children flood into the streets

Lloyd Rowe, Stockport, Cheshire

THE ARGUMENT

The clock, the music, the tears,
Unhappiness, self-pity, your fears.
Alone with no conversation, no smile,
Left only with your brain to accuse, confuse, and bring
Denial.

Alone with silence and boredom,
Slowly reaching your final decision.
Shut away in your boxed space,
Able to think, plan, and contemplate.

Why did it happen? Why are you here?
They don't want any hurt or any fear.
Ignore your pride, realise your mistake,
Two apologies, two smiles, two joined hands in a shake.

Emily Fozard, Huntington, Cheshire

REDUNDANCY

From lung-capped
To cracking her ribcage
With one sentence.
Letting scarlet words pour
Straight to the heart
As translucent blood begins
To saturate her corded
Dark green carpet.

She's let her pen run away with her,
Always travels with it caressing her
Methodically slicing her open,
Her pen-knife.

Performing autopsies on her life.
Among her scripted organs
(Those events that dye her soul)
She writes and asks the question
Will these poems ever make
Redundancy worthwhile?

Sara Campbell-Kelly, Macclesfield, Cheshire

Born in Manchester, **Sara Campbell-Kelly** has interests
including art, music and writing. "I started penning verses
in my young teenage years as a way of venting emotions,"
she explained. "My work is influenced by my life, music,
empathy, humour and circumstance, and I would describe
my style as humorous, empathetic, autobiographical and
observational. I would like to be remembered as a happy
person." Aged 23, Sara is self-employed. "I have written
around 300 poems and have had several of them published," she added.

OVERTAKING MY OWN LIFE

Another short day is driving the vintage car in front,
My longer life will have become shorter by tonight,
So he beckons me past with a subtle wave of authority,
The road he sees is clear for the foreseeable future.

People can annoy me to that breaking point
Where I verbally explode,
Common sense of crude with no ability
To be charmingly rude,
Like the toffee-nosed smart arse
Sniffing the seat of your pants,
The on pedestal hell raising heroes,
Long overdosed, coming up clean,
From anger management classes amid rehab publicity.

A shock to the system slows you down
To a more leisurely pace,
Don't want to get by, but life's ahead still waving me past,
Overtaking my own life on the left
As flashbacks fly by on the right.

Stephen Flinn, Crewe, Cheshire

BASKETS OF LINEN

I glance over my shoulder and see
A woman carrying a basket.
A woman carrying a basket.

In the basket is a bundle of linen.
I continue walking and do not look back.
And although I do not know this woman
I have given her a name.

The next morning I have forgotten her,
Yet now, when I see a basket of linen
I am reminded of that time when
I glanced over my shoulder and saw
That woman, carrying a linen basket.

And with each time I see her,
She has grown a little older,
A little slower, a little paler:
A little slower, a little paler,
A little older.

Kevin O'Brien, Warrington, Cheshire

ROMANTIC

Low the sun lies in the sky,
Beset with clouds illuminated,
By the touch of varied dye.

Lo, the evening, calls to me,
To hear the blackbird's lullaby,
Fade to the distance, quietly.

Though this causes me to feel,
Similar sensation aroused by thee,
Nature's love is never so real.

So it is I see, most certainly.

Kylie Scott, Alsager, Cheshire

MERSEY MAGIC

When people ask me where I'm from, I'm very proud it's
clear,
Oh I was born in Liverpool and still live very near.
You must know both our football teams and great singers
like The Beatles,
I tell them more about the port, the pride of local people.
Walk along the Pier Head, find the buildings called three
graces,
Look up at a Liver bird and see which way it faces.
Five theatres, two cathedrals, Albert Dock and the muse-
ums,
However long you stay with us, do make sure you see
them.
So visit Liverpool, book some tickets, make a date,
For our capital of culture in two thousand and eight.

Elizabeth Galvin, Neston, Cheshire

AT TIMES I FEEL DOWN

At times I feel down,
Like I have no soul,
Is this me,
For the rest of eternity?
For eternity is what I feel is what is ahead of me.
Forever bored.
Forever listless,
Forever indifferent and unable,
Another day after another day,
Piling up on top of one another,
Until one day a
Collapse, and life is over,
Life is gone.

Darren Thomas Heath, Winsford, Cheshire

SONNET FOR CHELSEA

Chelsea for gardens with exquisite themes
Fashionable ways to arrange your own plots
Yet strangely romantic with scenic dreams
And this year poignant with war memoir slots
Digging for victory to raise homely greens
While in the peace garden, peacefully flows
Pure water from peace walls, in silver sheens
And there, named Remember, blooms a white rose

Cheer for the great pavilion blazing
Of scarlet and pink, orange tones and blue
Some of your favourites in shades amazing
Clematis and Iris in colours new

Chelsea for partners and Chelsea for chums
Chelsea for each garden lover who comes

Margaret Hoole, Winsford, Cheshire

THE EAGLE

With wings outstretched across the skies
The eagle to its eyrie flies
On those same wings its young are carried
As the new chick frets and tarries

When the time is right and ready
The precious chick grown and steady
The parent with sweet love and care
Withdraws to watch that first time dare

And with parental pride views o'er
The chick as it proceeds to soar
Off and away to seek a mate
Build its own eyrie work out its fate

Another scene we then may view
As gracefully and heart so true
With wings outstretched across the skies
The eagle to its eyrie flies

Annie Marsh, Widnes, Cheshire

Annie Marsh said: "A few years ago, I had the privilege of being high in the mountains of India. There we watched a vulture riding the thermals. When writing poetry I find myself influenced by many aspects of life and nature. *The Eagle* is based on a verse from the Bible, Exodus, chapter 19, verse 4. *...as an eagle carries her young on her wings...* When the young eagle is reticent about learning to fly, the parent will soar high with its young on her back. She then tenderly withdraws her support, enabling the fledgling to fly free for the first time."

THE MINER

He leaves his home where there's sun and light
And soon he turns his day to night
His lunch he carries in a pack
His shoulders round and humped his back
His face is drawn, both lean and grey
Each time while in the cage he'll pray
That no disaster will prevail
And that his courage will not fail
He's nearly six foot, really tall
Yet on his knees he has to crawl
Along a tunnel through the earth
You don't know what your coal is worth
His days are very dark and black
The scars of life show on his back
From proving all the skills he's learnt
To watch for gas, so he won't get burnt
His courage is just not his own
For he has friends, he's not alone
Working down there in that mine
In darkness where the sun won't shine

E Levy, Cheadle, Cheshire

MOON STREET

Dark of the night,
Walking round town,
Ready as we'll ever be,
Something's going down.

Straight out of a magazine,
Propping up the bar,
Leaving by the side door,
Starting up the car.

Woman in the moonlight,
Amber in the streetlight,
He's a strange one, over there,
Lighting up a cigarette,
People stop and stare.

Screaming kids and alley cats,
Waiting for the dawn,
The psychology of a midnight town,
On Moon Street were they born.

M C Jones, Chester, Cheshire

IF

If you were a flower
You would be a rose
If you were a colour
You would be a rainbow
If you were a bird
You would be a dove
If you were a feeling
You'd be pure love
You are all of these things
Rolled into one
You are the best
And you're my mum

G Ingram, Great Sutton, Cheshire

PHOTOGRAPH DAY

On photograph day we all stood
In rows, back on the boards
In the assembly hall
Our teeth chattering in the cold
Like the clocks ticking on the walls
Incessantly, becoming out
Of time with even themselves

We waited for a click that snapped
Suddenly and we were gone
Snatched from our senses, on
Display for some future's lost sight

I looked terrible, inevitably
Staring madly at the flash that snipped time
You flinched at the back

John West, Chester, Cheshire

LIFE

Life is a very difficult thing
Sorrows and many joys with it brings
It slips through your fingers like a wet bar of soap
Leaving you lonely, with nothing, no hope

It's a delicate thing and so are your friends
But with love, itself it mends
It soon disappears and flies up above
Taking you with it and all your past love

I won't go on much, but I really must say
Make the most of every day

Kate Helen Ogden, Altrincham, Cheshire

MY BABY

My baby cries, my baby weeps,
But most of the time my baby sleeps,
A baby sigh, a baby laugh,
My baby loves a baby bath,
Lots of colours, lots of light,
Ensures he gets a peaceful night,
Nice warm clothes and food to eat,
Is sure to keep my baby sweet,
What baby likes, then baby gets,
My baby never, ever forgets,
He likes to shout, he wants to play,
He loves to see me every day,
A nasty cough, a runny nose,
Ten little fingers, ten little toes,
One little smile, always brightens my day,
Maybe soon my baby will say,
Mamma.

Rosie Stanley, Widnes, Cheshire

SNOW

The snow settles softly on the slope,
So pure and white and full of hope.
The children laugh and love to play,
So pure and whole; at peace today.
The sun shines softly down on us,
We feel alive; a happy buzz.
We laugh and smile and sledge down hills,
So glad to have our simple thrills.
But soon the snow becomes awash,
And melts away like tears because;
The sun's too hot and the day too long,
And to laugh and hope and love is wrong.
We should have known it could not last,
Having hope will always pass.
And we are left with frozen toes;
Like love and life, snow comes and goes.

Jessica Williams, Sandbach, Cheshire

Born in Warrington, **Jessica Williams** has interests including mountaineering, running and travel. "I started writing poetry in my teens, because it was a good way to express my emotions without having to talk about them," she explained. "My work is influenced by the outdoors and people I love, and I would describe my style as simple. I would like to be remembered as a good person." Aged 23, Jessica has an ambition to own her own mountain centre in the hills and be surrounded by her friends.

REMEMBER

Always remember, never forget
What you give out in life, is what you get
Live your life to the full, as if each day were your last
Live in the present and not in the past
All the beauty around is yours for the taking
Open your heart for a new awakening
All the answers you want are all around
The simplest things are what I've found
We've only got one chance in life
So let's not waste it with arguments and strife
So always remember, never forget
What you give out in life is what you get
If you hand out sorrow and grief and woe
Please be assured, that is all you will know
The world all around will seem grey and dark
The forces invoked will leave their mark
So lift up your heart and hold out your hand
Say to yourself, ain't life grand
Rejoice in the fact that you are part of the plan
And bring love and peace to your fellow man

Kate Bevan, Warrington, Cheshire

ONE FOR SORROW, TWO FOR JOY

Two magpies settle on the road ahead,
The road to autumn and winter.
One picks at a glittering jewel,
Quickly at first, with gentle pecks.
But then more strongly, peck on peck,
In a frenzy of hammer blows.

She stands apart warily watching,
Not too close, but aware
Of his anguished battering,
Trying to say, I'm here, I'm here.
She tires, flies off, looks down
From the middle branches of a beech.

He stops at last, exhausted
Unable to prise the diamond
From its setting in the road,
He looks up, but she has gone.
The leaves of the beech are copper now,
Falling, falling, falling.

Ken Wild, Nantwich, Cheshire

LIES

All right, so I'm a liar, a pretender and a cheat,
You see the matter simply, cannot tolerate deceit.
Easier to agree that I'm all that you despise,
Than shambling, try to analyse,
The reasons for my lies.
Not content with the music that we shared,
Sensing something held back, some allegiance undeclared,
With lasers you blasted the sore I tried to hide,
Burned out the cancer, and destroyed our love beside,
But, Black Widow Spider,
Somehow I survived.

Alma Gardner, Cheadle, Cheshire

YOU ARE MY

You are my bronze on stone
You are my silver in my coppers
You are my treasures gold

You are my Berlin, buried in enemy lands
You are my shining beacon of light
You are my hope in Pandora's box

You are my glasses
You are my telescope
You are my inspiration

You are my one
You are my all
You are my best friend
In troubled times
This says it all

Stephen Beckett, Sandbach, Cheshire

LOCH LINNHE

Dissolved is night's draped shadowed cape.
Shade now expires where water mirrors day;
Beholds afresh the swell of dawn's jewelled face.

Clouds arouse, and stir from drowsy heights,
Suffuse in salmon light above the loch's embrace;
Soaks warm the sun's first flush of fluid space.

Far hills leer and brood their rolling girth;
Opaque their huddled limbs into the liquid east:
Resplendent blend of flame down echoed peaks.

Mike Penney, Chester, Cheshire

JETLAG

It's four in the morning,
Impossible to sleep,
A twelve hour flight,
Aurora lights
Keep me from the feat.

A cosy little hotel room,
Luggage sprawled in a heap,
Flying as high as a kite,
No sheep in sight,
Makes me want to weep.

Nine in the morning,
I just can't stay awake.
A long hard night,
I just can't fight,
I'm finally asleep.

Zoe Edmondson, Stockport, Cheshire

AUTUMN

Red, gold and bronze upon the floor
The papery leaves
Rustle as I wade through
The autumn's fall.
The grey-blue sky with solemn cloud
Hangs moodily above the trees,
The cool damp air
Is still.
Small birds dart in and out
Along the hedge,
A spider's web shimmers silvery threads
Hung with ivory beads.
A pheasant's call hollow from the woods.

Caroline Cliff, Nantwich, Cheshire

Born in Norbury, **Caroline Cliff** has interests including poetry, arts, crafts and growing plants. "I was inspired to write poetry by comedian and poet John Hegley and my work is also influenced by Victoria Wood," she explained. "My style can be serious or humorous depending on my mood, and my biggest fantasy is to live on a tropical island." Aged 40, Caroline is a health professional and is married to Phillip. "The person I would most like to be for a day is Richard Branson," she added.

THE BEACH

I walked upon the sandy beach and all around the seagulls
Screeched.

The endless tide crashed on the shore, leaving behind
Shells and seaweed galore.

Rocky outcrops here and there, children playing
Everywhere.

A bracing wind, the air so fresh one can hardly get their
Breath.

People swimming in the sea, others paddling near to me.

A distant ship on the horizon seen, I wonder where she's
Going or been.

Donkey rides and ice cream too, plenty here to occupy you.

Dogs run around upon the sand, there's so much space,
Isn't it grand.

Robert Laing, Stockport, Cheshire

PULL ME FROM THE FIRE

Pull me from the fire, my love
And keep me safe from harm
Shield me from the flames
And hold me in your arms

Save me from the embers
That burn so deep inside
And cool me in the waters
Of a foaming ocean tide

And though my soul may smoulder
My heart will slowly melt
And the words will flow more freely
Than the rage that I have felt

Then I will see more clearly
What your heart may desire
And my tears will fall so freely
As you pull me from the fire

A Wynne-Morter, Northwich, Cheshire

Dedicated to my wife, Dee for being there and believing in me.

THE SECRET OF THE MORNING

The fairies come at the break of dawn,
Their bright clothes shine all around,
They cry soft dew onto the dark grass,
And then leave with barely a sound.

They smile at us when we are sleeping,
They awake all the birds in the trees,
They sing softly to all the flowers,
And then they spread their tiny wings
To the breeze and leave.

Erin Story, Runcorn, Cheshire

LETTING GO

Peace, give me your shelter
Touch my eyes with quiet scenes of joy
Happy days flowing like a river
Dreams dancing in my sleeping head
Move me with grace and gentleness
To places where solitude no longer shades
The light from the path of my days
Calm, hold me in your hands
Carry all longings far away
On a sea of slow tranquillity
With secret lapping waves
Love makes me a better one
A person who smiles at life
Tears fall too easily each night
As if to wash away the doubts
Keep worries from my door
And let me lay my burden down

Anne Platt, Romley, Cheshire

THE MASK

Behind the mask, a hidden face
A tear to trace
A face of fear, a call to here
Behind the mask, I am so brave
A hope to save

Behind the mask, the eyes so cold
Too young to be so old
Behind the mask, is where I stay
All my troubles go away

Ann Fielding, Sale, Cheshire

DANCE WITH THE GODS

The music of the pipes, trills through the air
Favonius cavorts beneath the budding boughs
Where birds carol the change from winter to spring

Come, dance with the gods this spring

Flora drifts amongst the hedgerows
Replenishing the wine of the gods, in their golden chalices
Awakening the plant life to the year's cycle of growth and
rebirth

Come, dance with the gods this spring

Has the music of the pipes bestirred you?
Or is winter's dormant phase still within?
Harken to the symphony, bury winter's sloth and sin

Come, dance with the gods this spring

J Dyson, Chester, Cheshire

YOU

I knew you were there, I could feel you but not see you,
Smell you, but not heed you,
You were there with magical grace,
I could see your mind, but not your face,
I carry on knowing that you are there,
Don't know how and I don't care,
It was you, you, you were there,
I know it's you, no one else can compare.

Emma Jane Brookes, Sale, Cheshire

Born in Crewe, **Emma Jane Brookes** has interests including reading, writing, line dancing, swimming and ice-skating. "My step-father is a poet and gives me inspiration," she explained. "I would like to be remembered as a gifted writer and my ambition is to write a bestseller and act in the film of it." Aged 30, Emma works as an administrative assistant. "I am currently writing a novel and have written short stories and countless poems. The person I would most like to meet is the rapper Eminem, to find out how he thinks of his rhymes," Emma added.

EIGHT TWELVE EIGHTY

That timeless sound
With lyrics of deepest wonder
A life
Fought with rage
For an ever powerful peace

John Lennon
Fallen down
Staining this carpet of awe
His heart pricked
By thorn of bloody rose

Those frozen fingers
Of death
Reach out and touch
But
Petals of love gently fall
And this bloody rose
Is no more
On this mourning
Numbed
In silent disbelief

June Metcalfe, Warrington, Cheshire

A SPECIAL FRIEND

Laying in bed, all swollen with mumps,
Feeling really fed up and down in the dumps.
Everywhere aches, even readings a chore,
As my eyes are all puffy, it's such a bore.

It was great at first being off school,
I didn't imagine I'd be ill at all.
I knew I'd catch it from my best friend,
Now I'm laying here and she's on the mend.

Then in comes dad, puts a box on the bed,
I ease myself up, with a thumping head.
Lift the lid slowly. Gasp! Eyes all agog.
Out pops a ginger waggy tailed dog.

Is it for me, this bundle of fluff?
Dad smiles and nods, the puppy says wuff.
Mumps all forgotten, nothing matters at all.
From that day on, Bob and me, are inseparable.

Valerie Wyatt, High Lane Village, Cheshire

*Dedicated to my dad, the original song and dance man, so
full of fun.*

HEARTBREAK

Through my telescope, I can see a beach
And on that beach, I can see a woman
On that woman, I can see a wedding dress
And on that wedding dress, I can see dirt and cuts

Her feet are damp from the sea
And her face is soaked from the tears which
Pour, crushingly, down her cheeks
In her mind she's broken-hearted

Sophie Bradburn, Crewe, Cheshire

DESTINY

I am what will be, what mysteries lie in store
I am the path on which no one has trod before
I am what follows, in darkness and in light
The world as it will be, your blindness is my sight,
Hidden in the shadows, I await the call
On the edge of humanity, I predict the fall
Reach out into nothingness and I will be there
Waiting to entice you into my lair
Over stormy waters, see me stalk my prey
Hungrily watching, as ships go astray
In the darkening skies I'll be waiting for you
Tread lightly my friend, I need new flesh to chew
I am the path of what will be
You have no choice but to follow me
I am your eyes, but I see more
Each step you take brings you closer to my door
I am reality, I am the end you see
You must believe in me, I am your destiny

Karen Cottriall, Leasowe, Cheshire

THE STORM

A storm screams down from the sky at midnight.
I wake myself seeking signs of morning.
A shadow spreads across the streets in the dim light.
The stoic streetlamp is a beacon of warning.

A faceless voice screams out from the thunder.
I rise high and feel the blow of its bright sword.
The fear and the venom in the vent split asunder.
The tears of defeat, from the eye of the night lord.

Rob Coker, Winsford, Cheshire

PAST AND PRESENT

Where are the days when kids used to pray?
Thanking the Lord for a lovely day
Where are the days of rock and roll?
When Georgie Best scored every goal
Where are the days when wicked meant bad?
Now it means good- the world's gone mad.
Where are the days of the corner shop?
And teenagers enjoyed the Saturday hop.
Where are the days of the gramophone?
Margaret Lockwood and Franchot Tone.
No longer on these thoughts I will dwell
Was life in those days really so swell?
We now have dish-washers and fast moving trains
And antibiotics to cure all our pains.
We have digital hearing for the very deaf,
Motels, McDonalds, The Little Chef.
The past has gone, the future unfolds,
We may question what the future holds.

Lesbia Mary Shone, Little Neston, Cheshire

CONVERSATION

Two crows sat on a gate one day
Both meant to leave without delay
Discussing when and how quite soon
But stayed on talking late through June

As each in thought had more to say
The problem grew till autumn day
Wore on through winters sleet and snow
Where each departure failed to show

Spring came early with restrain
The more they talked and talked again
This fond dilemma must end soon
For once again we are in June

Each timely season came and went
The longer they in conference spent
And never once a pause for rest
They just got better than their best

Till nature had their flight in shore
Let not a word be uttered more
When crack between a verbal noun
The gate at last had fallen down

Michael Corroboy, Warrington, Cheshire

Michael Corroboy said: "I have been writing children's verse and illustrating my own work for the last 25 years, with some success in magazines and the local press. I attended both Manchester and Liverpool art schools and have continued painting watercolours throughout my life. At the moment I have over 200 children's poems written, unpublished, unseen and prepared, only to be read."

JUSTICE IS SERVED

Do you remember all the times
I said, "I love you,
I'll always forgive you,
No matter what you do?"
Well, guess what
My dear, I lied?
It's time to salvage
Some tattered pride.
Your suits are snipped,
The car's a wreck,
Credit is debit,
And you'd better check,
The web for that tape you hid,
I'm selling it,
For the highest bid.
So farewell, my darling,
Don't worry, I'll call.
We'll meet again...
In the courts of law.

Pauline Leung, Great Sutton, Cheshire

DUSTING WHILST WATCHING THE LONDON MARATHON

They're off.
Setting the pace,
Running the race,
Hoping to shake the weary hand of history.
Looking on, I let my duster fall,
And for a moment, feel the same confused
Response I always feel
When someone gives something their all.
My father's words revisit with a rush,
Just do your best before it really is too late,
And he was right,
But all experience is a subtle state of
Our decisions and the ever-open palm of fate.
What should we do with someone else's silver cups,
Certificates and honourary ties?
Who knows what thought is passed from hand to mind,
What we could find if we found time?
I dust them carefully, put them in place,
And suddenly, I realise, his race was run
For me.

Claire Morton Bull, Macclesfield, Cheshire

*Dedicated to Leslie Hough, who was a very good father and
a wonderful friend.*

FREEDOM

I will run with the sun as each day is begun,
I will soar with the birds in the sky.

I will laugh at the world 'neath my dancing feet,
And completely forget how to cry.

Janet Swindells, Chester, Cheshire

RACISTS

They call us names, a callous trait
These bunch of thugs, consumed with hate
They claim this land, to be their own
And say "Leave now, just go back home"

The old or young, they just don't care
Such verbal abuse, is it really fair?
Whatever names they choose to call
Their worthless words, we've heard them all

We shall ignore their foul-mouth tongue
And to this land, we do belong
We're born and bred, that is, UK
This beautiful home, is where we'll stay

So let's fight on and don't dismay
Racists live on, they're here to stay
Let's stand together, unite we must
Against those bigots, their cause unjust

Christian Kantel, Denton, Cheshire

EMPTY SEAT

There is an empty seat in the café today,
Has the lovely old lady passed away?
The waitress wonders. Over the years, she
Has not missed a morning, but hold the tears,
A rival café has lowered its price
On a pot of tea and vanilla slice.

Gary Darbyshire, Warrington, Cheshire

BIRDWATCHER

The little boat glides out of the reeds,
Silently over the water.
The man watches a heron as it feeds:
He could easily have caught her.

Putting binoculars to his eyes,
He scans water and land around:
Birdwatcher, he sees a bird as it flies,
Later, he sees it on the ground.

Interested in birds from foreign lands,
With odd plumage, strange sounding names.
When caught, on their legs are put certain bands,
Gently, so that none of them lames.

He spends many hours as still as the grave,
Studying birds and their strange ways,
Finding out which endangered species to save,
So they can survive future days.

J Millington, Northwich, Cheshire

TWO BLUE LINES

Can it honestly be really true?
Are there two line lines and they are blue?
I can't believe what I see there,
The joy I see is almost too much to bear.
And yet I still have a little doubt,
Although this is what my life is about.
Excitement, fear, fill my mind,
I never thought two blue lines I'd find.
If you have agonised like me,
Waited patiently results to see.
Has God at last my pleading heard?
Listened to every fervent word.
The miracle of life starts now in me,
I never thought this day I'd see.
But there it is, two lines of blue,
I can hardly wait till I see you.
To hold you close after all this time,
I love you so, little baby of mine.

Ann O'Brien, Altrincham, Cheshire

Ann O'Brien said: "I am an actress, singer and writer. I have been a soloist at weddings for the past 25 years, having also composed numerous commissioned theme songs. Over the last few years I have been asked to write bespoke poetry for brides and grooms, parents, grandparents and special occasions. I put into verse the feelings about a loved one, and their lives and special qualities. I have appeared on stage and TV and I delight in reading my poetry to the sick and old. I have recorded several CDs and am at present working on my first play. More details can be found at www.originalpoems.co.uk."

HANDS

I'm just a pair of hands
I don't do any harm
I spend my day just doing things
On the end of someone's arms

I comb your hair and brush your teeth
I even iron your clothes
Both together we wash your face
And sometimes pick your nose

You can't do nowt without me
You're stuck with us for life
I daren't begin to tell you
The times I've hugged your wife

But we're not that clever I have to say
And I admit we're not too bright
'Cos when you lose your temper
Its us that has to fight

So please don't let some fool tell you
That the heart is our queen bee
'Cos without a good strong pair of hands
Where would the midwife be

Graham Bowers, Gee Cross Hyde, Cheshire

FATHER TIME

He's a comforter and healer
Of whom you should beware
For streaks of silver lingered
Where his fingers stroked my hair

He came to me when father died
His touch as soft as silk
But later my complexion
Resembled curdled milk

My figure is much fuller now
Since he came of late
I think he sneakily slowed down
my metabolic rate

Whenever I was worried
He so kindly stroked my brow
And could you plant potatoes
In those furrows now

He caresses your life essence
And with expertise and stealth
He fortifies and heals and slowly
Takes it for himself

Amanda-Jane Lee, Cheadle, Cheshire

FEAR OF THE GHOSTS

I came to this place to get away,
But, what a fool I have been,
To believe that it would not repeat again,
Isolation and neglect is what I feel.
The past has come to haunt me,
I came to this place to get away,
But now my ghosts have found me.

Nic Colquitt, Northwich, Cheshire

THE GIRL BEHIND THE COUNTER

Our encounter that morning was brief
I passed over my wares
She did not look back but stared in grief
And with some pain that I could never share

Her lank hair hung on her forehead
Its fringe forming a shield
Behind which she could shelter and hide
From life and any happiness it might yield

On two of her fingers was a bandage
To protect against what new injury
That life had dealt at her tender age
I could not tell, but I wanted to say sorry

And hold her like a parent would
And give her the courage to face
A world that can be cold
And love barely leaves a trace

John Duncan, Macclesfield, Cheshire

JOY

Joy,
I remember the feeling
The leaping of heart and quickening of breath.
The upward surge of the spirit towards heaven.
Will I ever feel this again
Now that I am old, careworn and sad.
Life has taken my joys and tossed them up on the beach,
Lost, bedraggled and oh, so fragile.

Linda Jackson, Nantwich, Cheshire

ODE TO TWO GLASS GOBLETS

Spirits of earth and water
Captured forever in a glass.
Twin goblets of great beauty,
Each with its own unique theme.

Blue for the water and sea,
With great black fishes embossed.
Swimming in endless life span
Without storms to trouble your way.

Brown for the life giving earth,
With creatures so dark and bold.
Captured as timeless as you live,
No hunter to fear as you go.

When sunlight shines through your bowls,
All beauty is revealed.
What pleasure and joy you give,
As all creation you show.

Doreen C Nall, Chester, Cheshire

SMOG

Pale, pallid sun, damp still air,
O'er water silent, mist drifts down,
The city wrapped in blanket black,
Knitted by ten thousand fires.

Soon silence rains, as hasty traffic stills,
Reluctant sightless drivers quit,
The empty trams, abandoned sit,
Till, no choice, the trek begins.

Street lamps dimmed, their friendly glow,
Markers for the wraiths below,
Masked by scarves in vain, to muffle,
Seeking clues they homeward shuffle.

Looming shapes, the memory disturbs,
Confused, uncounting lurking kurbs,
Combine, till watery eyes, discern at last,
A sign directing to a welcome latch.

Stained masks removed, clogged mucous cleared.
Two days, a breeze, no more to fear,
Soot dispersed, the city springs to life,
Except for those frail lungs, that failed the strife.

Reg D Drew, Northwich, Cheshire

WHEN YOU'RE NOT HERE

The air that surrounds me is freezing cold
When I'm all alone, it's only you I want to hold
I try to keep warm but its just not the same
When you're not here in my mind, it rains

There's an empty space on the right of me
I know exactly what's missing and who it should be
Seconds tick by, ten times slower than time
When you're not here, right next to my side

The sky turns darker and clouds don't fade
I look down at a bed that's freshly made
I climb in and close my eyes really tight
The only person I want to dream of is you tonight

When I wake up I can feel you beside me
I open my eyes but emptiness is all I see
I feel a cold shiver shoot right up my spine
As I realise what I felt was just in my mind

I curl back up into my small cocoon
Spend the rest of the night alone in my room
Every single thought in my head is of you
As I close my eyes and imagine everything we do

Emma Wilson, Boughton, Cheshire

WHEN SPRING COMES ROUND AGAIN

It's been a long, cold winter.
Chill winds that penetrate,
The warmest padded jacket.
But Spring was worth the wait.

To see the first buds open,
And hear the blackbird sing,
Has cheered us all and given hope:
New life in everything.

We open up our windows,
To let the sunlight shine,
Through all the darkest corners,
In your home, and in mine.

Each year brings aspirations,
Of all we hope to do.
If you're like me, they'll still remain,
Undone, the whole year through!

We promise to do this and that;
Draw plans: make lists and then,
Decide to wait till next year,
When spring comes round again.

Eve Armstrong, Warrington, Cheshire

EASTER

Twigs a sprig and buds abound,
Blooms and blossoms all around.
Time has come for easter ballad,
Lighter clothes, and things with salad.

In field and copse and avenue,
The flora's burgeoning anew.
'Neath undergrowth and forest floor,
Fecundity is rife once more.

Word is spread by bleat and whinny,
Over valley, heath and spinney;
'Midst the feathers, 'midst the fur,
Fertile union does occur.

Signs of spring the young exhibit,
Lambs a frolic, frogs a ribbit.
If, or not, they're acrobatic,
Birds and bees and beasts are at it.

Chirps and chirrups by the earful,
Are good reason to be cheerful.
Nature spruced and at it's best,
Ready for the easter fest.

Shirley Brierley, Hyde, Cheshire

RHYTHMIC THINKING

Where are you going to on your chosen path?
Are you going to make a difference?
Are you trying to make your way?

What? I? What do you mean?
I just want to be me

But how? How are you going to be you?
What do you want to achieve?

I want to be noticed and not be a number,
I want to give you all I have to give.

To give, but how?
You need to know how,
You need to set some goals.

I have goals, many goals,
But how are they to be achieved?

Goals you may have,
But do you realise them?

No, not I, I can't see how,
How do I make them real?

You act upon them, make them real,
That's my friend, how you make your mark.

Anna Marie Goodwin, Hyde, Cheshire

UNTITLED

You were born in February of nineteen ninety eight,
For you to grow up so big, I could hardly wait.

But now the time has flown and you've grown so fast,
I long for you to be small, to cradle you like in the past.

You're growing and learning with each passing day,
And your personality shines through in every way.

You are like Mummy and daddy, but most of all,
You're just you.
You're clever, unique and remarkably pretty too.

How proud I am to know that you're a part of me,
Just to think of you makes me smile with glee.

And as you grow, more happiness you bring,
I love to watch you sleep, play, dance and sing.

If I could I would bottle every last moment,
To look back when I wonder where the time went.

But darling I will never need to do that,
because in my head and in my heart,
Is where you will always be at.

You will always be my baby,
Even when adulthood has come,
And my precious, I'll always be your mum.

C Newton, Crewe, Cheshire

Dedicated to Brianna-Janel, the one who made my life complete, my precious diamond, I will love you always. From Mummy.

YOU

Somebody get me off this ride,
My soul is churned up inside.
The ground I walk on looks likely to subside,
Can't tell what's right in my own mind.

Somebody get me out of here,
I'm cold and alone, insincere.
I need a place where I don't feel weird,
A place, away from here.

Somebody get me out of this mess,
The pain I feel is causing distress.
What I need is a change of address,
And to get away from the daily stress.

Somebody saved me from all of this,
Somebody saved me with a kiss.
Somebody warm and kind and true,
Somebody, someone, you.

Steven Green, Stockport, Greater Manchester

Born in Stockport, **Steven Green** has interests including
writing, films and reading. "I think writing is in my blood
and my work is influenced by everything and everyone," he
remarked. "I would describe my style as eclectic because I
don't have a specific theme." Aged 30, Steven is a clerical
worker with an ambition to write, direct and produce his
own work. "The person I would most like to meet is Steven
Spielberg because he fires my imagination, and the person
I would most like to be for the day is the invisible man," he
added.

NANA

I was her favourite and I loved her so,
But her time was up and she had to go.
Nearly every day I think of her,
With a beautiful smile and skin so fair.
My nana meant the world to me,
From bone china she would drink her tea.
If only I could see her just one more time,
That would be so divine.
Not just to see but to hold her tight,
And talk to her for just one night.
She knows I love her with all of my heart,
Even though we're still apart.
I know the love bond still goes on,
Even after our loved ones have gone.
Their spirits draw near us every day.
And try to encourage us in every way.
Now I carry on with pride,
Knowing she is there by my side.
I love you nana I always will,
We'll meet again when my heart stands still.

Diane Heyes, Wigan, Greater Manchester

STREAM

A million thoughts run down this stream
Dreams drift away in these waves
I wonder if we have a life or were just slaves
Whatever happened to all those things we craved
And as I look at my reflection on the water's top
I think to myself, where will this stream stop?

James Kavanagh, Salford, Greater Manchester

IN PURSUIT OF A RECORD

She sails from the harbour all on her own,
To meet with the elements as yet unknown
To set sail round the world in storm and in calm
Sailing ever onward with many a qualm
For seventy one days she battled the oceans alone
With only the voices of her team mates at the end of a
phone
Voices coaxing and willing her on when all but
Determination and hope and gone
Masts that are broken and waves that collide, all these
Hazards she took in her stride
She wept with frustration and her sleeping was restless
and light
But sailed ever onward the record in sight
Crossing the finish to the sound of the gun, give up a cheer
the record is won
She sails up the channel in one final tack the people on the
shore are waiting to welcome her back
So raise up your glasses to Ellen
She's back

Leonard Walton, Swinton, Greater Manchester

LOVE SPELL

Warm embrace for winter night
Faithful wings for tender flight
An end to tears that fall like rain
Protection from unwanted pain
Romantic haze to blind all blue
Just add me, just add you

Joanna Webster, Swinton, Greater Manchester

THE BOY WHO RUINED CHRISTMAS

It's only now I realise why,
You should never eat a purple mince pie,
I think it had festered since Christmas last,
A shrivelled pastry shell charged with methane gas.

The company coming won't know what will hit them,
A smell so deadly it's far from heaven,
I'd buy some spray but the shops are all shut,
Oh God, stop the bubbling deep in my gut.

I haven't seen my uncle for seven years,
And the first thing I'll do is reduce him to tears,
It won't be tears of laughter nor sadly, tears of joy,
More like tears that sting, what's wrong with this boy?

I wish I hadn't been so hungry so near to the meal,
If only I'd waited and savoured something real,
Though the size of the turkey only adds to the notion,
That what will result is a more potent potion.

Neil Simms, Stockport, Greater Manchester

HAPPINESS SHOULD FILL OUR HEARTS

A key hidden deep inside,
Yearn to seek and you will find.
Laugh, show, spread truth your light,
An open chest puts up the fight.

If concealed, wrapped, locked away,
A penalty of sadness you will pay.

Newborn infant, a gift of life,
Praise from those who share in delight.
First words, steps, that cheeky smile,
A chosen name will be kept on file.

If concealed, wrapped, locked away,
A penalty of sadness you will pay.

Glee in eyes, shining big smile,
Portray your love, not denial.
An expression, gesture, acts of fun,
The goal to succeed can be fully won.

If revealed, unwrapped, not locked away,
A result of happiness you will gladly pay.

Chantelle Walker, Bolton, Greater Manchester

Chantelle Walker said: "I have been expressing my thoughts and feelings through poetry from the age of seven. My main influence is my surroundings. I believe that the best way to express emotions of either happiness or sadness is to create a deep, thoughtful verse, extremely powerful to the reader by use of strong imagery. This is my first poem to be published. Now my aspiration is to write many moreand have my own collection of published poetry for people to remember me by and mark my name as a successful author."

HEARTBREAK

Have you had your heart broken
Did you feel the pangs of emotion.
Was the pain too severe to endure
Did you want to tell for a cure.
Or maybe run and hide
To crush the sadness and tears inside.
Would this passion never dissipate
Lend a little peace to alleviate.
Did your friend lend a reluctant ear
In fear of a saddening tear.
Think your heart will never mend
Did you falsely smile, try to pretend.
Pray for the sun to shine.
And find your heart an anodine.
Were you glad to slumber to weep in peace
Wake and pray all had ceased.
You thought the morrow would kill the sorrow
Oh why it hurts so, that heartbreak blow.
There is no cure for a broken heart
Only love will repair that broken part.

Alan Green, Rochdale, Greater Manchester

CIGARETTE ADVERT

The tiny things and tinny throat-held excellence
Splash the pictures in jerky, withheld, fruit static
Skinned, up night ache vertices
Held up in smoke
In unionised state
With head held for puncturing

David Faggiani, Chorlton, Greater Manchester

THE SMALL CRUCIFIX

Realised did I, that I needed to act.
I couldn't keep putting it off any longer.
I could hear the knocking at my door.
Feel you knocking on my very heart,
Asking to come into my life.
And now I realise that you have always been knocking,
Only now, I can truly hear you.

I walk closer to the door, with the small
Crucifix in front of me.
I have denied you
Too many times, but now I am ready.

With a deep breath, I open the door for you.
Two candle flames in front of me flicker
And I gaze down at the small crucifix.
It's time to let you into my life,
And get to know you as
You've always known me.

David Lobodzinski, Manchester

?

O to be free of this earthly shackle,
To soar free into the vastness of space.
Cleansing the soul in the coldness between the stars,
Journeying into,
Forever, searching
Hoping to find an answer,
The reason for it all.

Albert Leonard, Stockport, Greater Manchester

A SPECIAL MOMENT

A love so tender,
A beauty so true,
A special moment
Shared only with you.

Your lips so tender,
Your smile so true,
A special moment
Shared only with you.

Wiping away my tears so tender,
I open my heart so true,
A special moment
Shared only with you.

A devotion so tender,
A friendship so true,
Many special moments
I only want to share with you.

Sabiné Ridge, Prestwich, Greater Manchester

LATE SUMMER

A clamour of children
And a hot sun
The best of summer.
This heat, long-parched for,
Thwarted by glare
Of a long winter,
Then furious winds
Of a reluctant spring,
Is healing.
Like children and flowers,
We lift our faces
To the sun,
But our rejoicing is different.
Sting of memory,
Sharp assurance
Of another winter
Give to present heat
A richer bite.
Flowers, unaware
Live in the anchored moment,
Innocent children,
Magically content
Breathe a careless joy.
Our gladness, rinsed
With experience, mature
With partial pain,
Is doubly precious.

Elsie Hamilton, Failsworth, Greater Manchester

Born in Manchester, **Elsie Hamilton** has interests including reading and writing correspondence. "I started writing poetry as a child and gradually began to use it to express my emotions and thoughts," she explained. "My work is influenced by nature, friends and situations and I would like to be remembered in friendship by those I know and love." Aged 82, Elsie is a retired teacher. She is the widow of James. "The person I would most like to meet is my long-suffering MP who I often write to about political issues," added Elsie.

ESCAPED

The mind is confused deep dark and lonely.
Isolated struggling to find answers.
The journey has begun to sort out this mind of mine.
It's a sad place its scary its not a safe place in this mind of
Mine.
Safety is needed but tricks are there trick of the mind will
Not be fair.
Torment madness restlessness tiredness takes over but
Sleep is not there.
The mind moves on struggles to be fair oh this tired mind
Of mine.
Sleep at last resting the mind sleeping tablets taken to rest
The torment in the mind.
Pills are needed to master the tricks of the lonely confused
State of this mind of mine.
Tablets taken thing are clearing like a clear blue sky.
No more fearing in this positive place of mine.
No more tablets the mind is getting stronger happiness is
Needed in this mind of mine.
Different ways of thinking how to make the mind clear
Freedom at last.

Beverly Beaumont, Manchester

STANDSTILL

Sometimes I feel I'm in a world of my own,
Where everything is grey and nothing has grown.
Time has stood still and the world has stopped,
The sun has gone out and the moon has dropped.
People standing still not moving at all
The day-light has gone and the stars start to fall.
Or maybe it's me I'm going out of my mind
So I'm drawing my curtains and closing my blind.

Graham Scotson, Bury, Greater Manchester

A FATHER FIGURE

The whispers of a morning chill
Shudder through the air
A vision of a lonesome child
Who no-one gives a care

Lies amongst the debris
Of a bitter life so cold
The remains of once a happy dream
Are battered worn and old

But suddenly some hope appears
A candle in the night
This hero needs no shiny shield
Or vicious sword to fight

He takes my hand and leads me home
Who is this man I see?
A rescuer he truly is
A man who resembles me

Daniella McLenaghan, Bury, Greater Manchester

HAPPY PHOBIA

I am happy when the day is sunny,
Like a fan is glad when his team is winning,
Like the sun is merry when it is blazing hot,
Like a tiger is joyful when it is hunting,
Like a bird is overjoyed when it is singing,
Like a book is blessed when it's pages are turning,
Like a cake is delighted when it's candles are burning,
I am happy when the day is sunny.

David Grant, Sale, Greater Manchester

WAITING GAME

I waited for your call today
Just like I waited yesterday
I still believe you when you say
This time you've truly changed

I waited for your call today
Whilst searching for a way to pray
Hoping this time, you would stay
But have you truly changed?

I waited for your call today
I think I may have found a way
To hurt you, even make you pay
In case you haven't changed

I waited for your call today
Just like I waited yesterday
Should I believe you when you say
This time you've truly changed?

Lisa Smith, Failsworth, Greater Manchester

FREE AS A BIRD

Perching on the window-sills to peep,
At children in their beds asleep.
Chirping and tapping on the glass pane,
Wake up sleepy heads it's morning again.
Off I would fly, all gardens to explore,
Flowers, trees, ponds and lots more.
Something to eat, bits of cake and toast,
Oh and worms, I like them the most.
With my friends I will chirp and play
Hoping the nasty cats stay away.
Flying through the trees, at nests I nosey,
Seeing if the babies are snug and cosy.
So much life goes on in trees
Squirrels, caterpillars, butterflies, bees.
Up in the clouds and the big blue sky,
Round and round, up and down I fly.
Time to splash and bath, that feels good,
This is my life, wouldn't change if I could.
I am a sparrow and this is my world
Life is great, I'm free as a bird.

Joan Dawson, Bolton, Greater Manchester

Dedicated to my tutor, Tracy Holroyd, for giving me inspiration and confidence to write, and for her encouragement and support.

Born in Salford, **Joan Dawson** has interests including writing, gardening, reading and walking. "I started writing poetry 10 years ago for my grandchildren, and my work is influenced by creative writing classes," she remarked. "I would describe my style as a mixture of feelings and I would like my poetry to be something which my grandchildren remember me by." Aged 62, Joan is retired. She is married to Robert and they have a son and daughter. "I have written short stories and many poems. My biggest fantasy is to be famous and acknowledged through a special achievement," added Joan.

INTERNAL TRIAD

I talked to me,
And then to me, around the camp fire glowing,
What seemed to be a core of fear,
was shimmering and growing.
I cried with me,
I laughed with me.
The picture's coming clearer.
We are a team,
Though we haven't been.
Now we're getting nearer.
My drama queen,
My pious nun, my higher self
Together.
A healing sigh,
A smile so wry.
Let's travel on forever.
I turn to me,
And then to me
The excess fears receded,
lets make a pact to travel back
Whenever it is needed.

Rosemary Hawes, Manchester

THE JOUSTING KNIGHT

Climbing on my horse, dressed up in shining clothes,
I have a strong feeling I'm going to win.
My heart is pounding with fear and excitement,
Confidence coming to my head, I get myself focused.
We get ready to charge,
I look at my opponent, my horse gets ready,
I scrape my lance against his metal chest
As I knock him off and win the game.

Kelly Horsfall, Prestwich, Greater Manchester

DANCING

We are dancing on your grave
Spinning around like whirling dervishes
Our arms stretched out above our heads
And our dresses billowing wide around our legs
As we dance upon your grave.
We are dancing on your grave
Two sisters, bound together by more than blood
By circumstance
How long have we waited to perform our dance?
It seems an eternity
But we need no rehearsal
No practising of our steps
Just our special stage
Your grave.
We are dancing on your grave
Resilient and happy, strong and together
And free at last
Free of you
As we dance upon your grave.

Jenni Edward, Rochdale, Greater Manchester

RECIPE FOR A PERFECT DAY

Take two or more small children
Add a great deal of patience
And a little make-believe.
Mix well with lots of laughter
Until some kisses appear
Carefully blend in plenty of sunshine.
Place mixture in a large green field
And bake till golden brown.

Kathryn Russell, Cheadle, Greater Manchester

MY GRAN

My granny is old and very stiff,
She moves slowly and uses her stick
To pick her way around her flat,
Especially when it comes to feeding her cat.

It meows and meows as the approaching smells,
Of fish entrails and horse gel
Come wafting over the kitchen sink.
Oops, the mat is askew,
And what do you think?

Poor granny has slipped, her stick in mid-air,
And landed on the cushions of air.
On top of her couch. which is just as well,
To avoid catastrophe and landing on Mel,
Her cat, who looks on in despair,
As granny retrieves her fly-away hair,
And laughs at her amusing plight,
While her cat sees his chance to take that first bite!

Pat McAleese, Prestwich, Greater Manchester

REFLECTIONS

As time goes by, I rue the day
Why so many distractions got in the way
There were games and toys and then there were boys
Dresses, tresses and generally messing
Rejections of course were seriously distressing
Hindsight is great
But I left it too late
I'm not on my own, so have my mates
If only we realised it was all on our plate
If I could turn back the clock and recoup all the years
I would settle for the pleasures that education brings men
Reaping the rewards of books and the pen

Catherine Coward, Rochdale, Greater Manchester

Dedicated to Harry, my lifetime companion and soulmate.

Born in Dublin, **Catherine Coward** has interests including
cycling, walking, reading and foreign travel. "My work is
influenced by life experiences and observations and I would
describe my style as pensive and reflective," she explained.
"I would like to be remembered as a caring, independent
and self-sufficient person." Aged 56, Catherine works as
an adult education lecturer in business and marketing and
has an ambition to have more time to write. She is married
to Harry.

REFLECTIONS

A mirrored face stares back at me,
A reflection,
The face others see.
But behind the smile a different scene,
Emotions, dreams, known to no-one,
No-one?
The me that I would like to be,
Free;
Free to run barefoot through sifting sand
With the wind in my hair,
Long flowing hair.
Dancing with veils of gossamer threads,
Rainbow hues,
Floating, drifting, swirling round,
Round.
Gliding between silken sheets
On a bed of scented down,
In love, in love.
Perhaps, one day, perhaps.
One face staring back at me,
A reflection,
The face others see.

Janet Garner, Stockport, Greater Manchester

MR ROMANTIC

He listens when I want to talk
He cooks me meals
We take a walk
When I am blue he holds my hand
I know he'll always understand
Just how I feel
It's no surprise
I see it all within his eyes

Christine Skeer, Manchester

THE CIRCLE

The circle closes ranks
Around a sea of white shirts with striped ties.
Haversacks of regulation
Weigh heavy on designer shoulders.
Polished shoes and perfumed socks,
Empty heads with dishwasher smiles.
Brain-waste briefcases,
Man-sweat fibres.
Ugly labels of tailored perfection,
Sat on concrete thrones.
Preferring faultlessness with smallpox
To the outcast with a grin.
Let the circle become broken
With hollow gaps and spaces
Let them slash their baggage contents
With no mercy or regret.
Sabotage the shackles of convention.
Meet themselves going forward
And let their lives begin.

Frances Rochelle Barrie, Prestwich, Greater Manchester

MY LOVE

Your hair is brown
Your eyes are blue.
I hold my whole life
Up to you.
You are my sun
And my moon.
My life in one
You are my love,
The only one.

Jessica Street, Denton, Greater Manchester

NEVER NEVERLAND

When I was just a little girl, bound tight within my pram
I realised that within this world, my mum was Peter Pan
She never took me by the hand or sat and read a book
Off she went to Neverland to play with captain Hook
Grown up life made her irate, I soon knew of my rank
'Cos she'd become a pirate and made me walk the plank
At least then I could swim quite free instead of being stuck
Until the captain saw me and caught me with his hook
Sometimes she was the crocodile and cried her daydream tears
But mainly she flew off a while to wash away her fears
I stayed in the Wendy house to care for the lost boys
They kept me there as their spouse to play with all their toys
If Tiger Lily would swap her part, then Pan would rescue me
But Tiger Lily knew from the start how to make Pan see
I dreamed of being Tinkerbell, then I could fly away
So I could leave this living hell, where I am forced to lay

Chris Smith, Atherton, Greater Manchester

UNTITLED

I went for a walk down Stockport
I saw the Mersey Square,
And the pigeons there all about sung in the air.
I saw the river Mersey
And got back at the market store
The town shopping centre
I like Stockport Square.
The post office old house sounded a bell
And sang aloud
And I like the River Mersey
I like Daw Bank.
I like Underbank
I like the shops
I saw a bus
It was going fast
Down Stockport Square
The bingo theatre
I caught a bus to Edgeley, the number eleven
I saw Edgeley at the County Square
They scored a goal.
The town Stockport is my favourite town.

Anthony Bardsley, Stockport, Greater Manchester

Born in Stockport, **Anthony Bardsley** has interests including writing, poetry, art, football and walking. "When I was 17 I felt the need to write and my work is influenced by John Lennon and Bob Dylan," he remarked. "I would describe my style as observation poetry and my ambition is to be a better poet." Aged 44, Anthony is single and the person he would most like to meet is Nelson Mandela. "My biggest fantasy is to go to New York and my worst nightmare is being stuck in a lift," added Anthony.

VISITORS

Memories filed past,
Ambling along the pathway,
Grey trench-coats and knotted scarves
Shuffling their feet,
Whispering conspiratorially
About their time here.

Hands in leather handles,
Swing the once then cumbersome cases
Or point to the many changes
Of by gone days.

So, on they'd carry
Smiling distantly
At those promised pleasures
That awaited them, each year.

But now,
The chill October wind
Clatters the boards
Against the windows,
And in the decaying recoil,
Only the winter's promise will be fulfilled.

Michael Bergin, Oldham, Greater Manchester

PRECIOUS SON

The fluttering heartbeat of a baby bird.
The softest caress of sweet breath.
A life as pure as the driven snow.
Skin as soft as silk.
Eyes, deep pools of clear water.
You lay beside me,
My heart is aching with love and pride.
My world.
My life.
My precious baby son.

Lesley Allsopp, Atherton, Greater Manchester

VAULTS OF STONE

Into the arms of Morpheus I creep
Down into the deep caverns of sleep.
Taking refuge in the unknown,
Safe in the imaginary vaults of stone.

Searching in the soft half light,
For a passage into the night.
There to contemplate alone,
In the imaginary vaults of stone.

Under the gaze of Hypnos, God of sleep,
With Morpheus waving dreams for me to keep.
I climb a peak from where wishes are thrown,
In the imaginary vaults of stone.

Now I reluctantly retreat,
With vines of hope and comfort clinging to my feet.
So I will return at a time unknown,
To the imaginary vaults of stone.

Michael Skeffington, Salford, Greater Manchester

RABBIT

I've been here for days you know,
Battered by wind, rain and snow.
And yet you see me every day,
As you traverse the motorway.
You never think what I once was,
My sprightly life destroyed because
You were late for work one day,
So all alone I'm forced to lay.
Deepest crimson marks my fur,
With a tyre mark for my sepulchre.

Ian Jenkins, Whitefield, Greater Manchester

THREE SILENT MINUTES

Three silent minutes as we glide upon the wind,
Then as we landed, D Day hell began.

The bridge we won and kept our grip upon,
The paras then dropped one by one.

Thousands landed, hundreds lived,
Soldiers drowned soldiers shot
Soldiers cried
"Is this our lot?"

Utah, Omaha, Gold, Juno and Sword
Names of beaches where men will never grow old.

Enemy waiting to greet us in hell,
Memories of this in our minds forever will dwell.

Three silent minutes, As we glided upon the wind.

Janice Brierley, Rochdale, Greater Manchester

HOSPITAL

The place of healing
Cleanliness perceived yet not proved.

Greasy hand marks clothe the bed rail
Needle covers and blood stained swabs lurk beneath
In a state of abandoned discard.

The sign on the wall doesn't fit
"Wash your hands" it says, quietly threatening.

Perhaps the appearance of clean hands
Will shame the clustering germs into a hasty exit

Instead of the patient.

Rosemary Chesters, Denton, Greater Manchester

Dedicated to my gorgeous daughter, Savannah Ariane, who fortunately survived the experience.

Rosemary Chesters said: "The whole concept of language, its flow, sound and written appearance, fascinates me. I am a synaesthete. I see words as colours, which adds a different perspective to my work. My creativity also finds expression in visual art forms. I employ language to discover what makes people tick, and then to try to encourage my thoughts and experiences into orderly and relevant formation as they spill onto the paper. I am a language addict and my love of writing expressed in various media both stimulates and soothes my mind, rather like my five children, who are my biggest works of creation."

THE NIGHT

Moving so fast
It's all hard to take in
But now I'm wondering
All this time, where you've been

While I wished for
Someone as perfect as you
I'll admit that I like you
Because frankly it's true

It seems so surreal
As though it's all been a game
But if we don't get on
Tell me then, who's to blame?

If it all turns out wrong
And we both get let down
Then I hope your smile stays
And you'll be around

But I'd love for it to work
And for it to feel right
I'm so nervous yet also
Can't wait for that night

Leanne McGing, Oldham, Greater Manchester

TICK, TOCK

The tick and the tock of the grandfather clock
As the pendulum swings.
The distant dull thud,
On the dark panelled wood,
And a bird outside sings.
The old antique chest, the chairs and the rest;
Remember these things,
For we won't be back here,
We'll be elsewhere next year;
Just remembering.

Jackie Connelly, Manchester

THE GRIM REAPER

Who is next on the Reaper's rota?
Who is next upon his list?
He has to meet his annual quota
And do not think that you will be missed.

It matters not if you're young or old
The tired old widow, the sprightly child.
The names come up and the bell is tolled
And he makes sure they are duly filed.

We have no means of really knowing
How soon or late we'll get the call.
What portion of our life's still owing
Before his axe is due to fall.

I hope he will grant me some more years
Even though my ninetieth grows near.

Ken Bradbury Harrop, Urmston, Greater Manchester

LET ME

Let me think,
Let me breathe,
Allow my heart to be relieved.
Don't want any drugs to calm me down,
Don't want to visit a busy town.
If only I could go for a country walk,
Or down by the canal,
No better still a gentle stream.
Somewhere I could get some peace
And have a pleasant dream
Just let me please.

Jo Rainford, Leigh, Greater Manchester

RED ROBIN

In the winter when it's cold and snow is in the ground,
On the window sill each morn, red robin will be found.
You will see him standing there, his red breast shining bright,
The only dash of colour in the wilderness of white.

Watch him pecking at the crumbs, how hungry he must be,
Then with the biggest piece of bread, he'll fly back to the tree.
In the nest his family, all wait with open beaks,
To satisfy the hunger with the good things that he seeks.

So from day to day he's there, gathering crumbs of bread,
Until at last, the winter goes and spring time comes instead.
So look out for red robin, in snow and ice and chill,
A-singing for his breakfast, upon the window sill.

Debbie Seddon, Urmston, Greater Manchester

NOVEMBER MOON

The cold November moon caught me off guard,
With its circular, shining and glowing façade.
Alone in the glare, awaiting a sign,
A secret, a whisper or a hush-a-bye rhyme.
A twig snaps close by, could this be the one,
Hinting that nature's night has begun?
Orchestral stars dance a pagan step,
Around the moon drapes a shimmering net.
Twinkling in rhythm to that mysterious song,
For the nocturnal creatures that sing along.
The conductor, a tree branch, swaying in time,
To lead in harmony, the darkness sublime.
Droplets of rain fall from the sky,
A percussive pitter-patter is heard nearby.
A whistling wind stirs through the trees,
The clapping of hands is mimicked by leaves.
The call of an owl cuts through the night,
A powerful crescendo upon taking flight.
As I make my way homeward for shelter and warmth,
The concert continues with birdsong at dawn.

Sarah Jane Price, Prestwich, Greater Manchester

Sarah Jane Price said: "This poem was inspired by my love of nature and how even as grown-up of twenty-six, I'm still in awe of its mysteries. I've been writing poetry, stories and lyrics since the age of eight and I have gone on to use this as a basis for my career as an actress and singer/songwriter. My ambition in life is to be successful and happy and to continue to use writing as a creative outlet for as long as I'm able."

IF A SPACEMAN LANDED

If a space man landed on earth today
I wonder just what he would have to say
With hatred and fighting everywhere
Nobody it seems to give a care

If he was to take a quick look round
Would he wish he's never touched down?
Would he see the bullet and the knife
And experience this world's endless strife?

If he's listened, perhaps he's hear
The falling of a silent tear
Shed in vain for those who died
Because of man's stupid pride

If he travelled from nation to nation
Meeting people of each generation
Would he despair for our children's lives,
Our mothers, fathers, husbands and wives?

If a space man landed on earth today
I guess I know what he would have to say
This world is not a fit and proper place
For a good, kind and intelligent race

Malcolm F Young, Dukinfield, Greater Manchester

DEATH

There is a man who comes to all
Dressed in black and fairly tall

It doesn't matter who you are
He'll come for you, no matter how far

You can't fight him, you're far too old
Before you know it, he's taken hold

And even if you take a poll
He'll come and steal your soul

Eric Taylor, Newton Heath, Greater Manchester

SHAMELESS PURSUITS

What are they?
Who has them?
Why are they so cold?
Why can't they be fulfilled?

They are the hopeless dreams.
They cannot find a place for you.
They are in control of those
Who play a significant part in life.

Pride is in their money.
Power is in their glory.
Prejudice is their choice.
Justice isn't their force.

They are the shameless pursuits,
Of those who cannot afford them.

Anantha Rudravajhala, Middleton, Greater Manchester

JACK 'A' DORE

We flew into a verve of grey,
That time I felled our winning stroke
By coveting her aviary.
Which labour woke my crow and spoke,
"You know you're always free to fly".
But lost outside, you'll come exempt,
deriding shallow reasons why.
So tumble in laughter at my attempts
To rid you of me.

Andrew Henderson, Stretford, Greater Manchester

Dedicated to Sarah.

A SUMMER'S DAY

The summer season is the one for me
All the leaves are on the trees

The grass is green, the days are bright
It doesn't go dark till late at night

Time for the barbie to be set alight

Sitting in the garden lazing around
An ice-cold beer on the ground

All our friends have come around
We discuss our problems, tell some jokes
While all the time the barbie smokes

Ladies with wine, men with beer
This is the best season of the year

Michael Buckley, Prestwich, Greater Manchester

ONE IN A MILLION

When God gives us friends
He only gives us the best,
He gave me you
Tolerance, patience and virtue.
All these you possess
A true friend
stands by you.
Through the rough
Smooth indifferent
Your smile lights
Up the room.
Your laughter echoes
You are a free spirit
You are one in a million.

Daniel Francis, Oldham, Greater Manchester

Born in Oldham, **Daniel Francis** has interests including
writing, music and natural history. "I joined a creative writing group in 1994 and have written consistently ever
since," he explained. "I would like to be remembered as a
person who contributed a lot of good to life." Aged 44,
Daniel works as a cleaner and has an ambition to run his
own creative writing group. "The person I would most like
to meet is the singer and songwriter Noel Gallagher
because his material is similar to my own," added Daniel.

BECOMING

Emotions running high
Highs, lows, ups, downs.
My highs are taking me higher,
My lows just took me down.
Emotions are running like wild fire,
I've got new and different thoughts.
The wire that held me down,
Is now beginning to crumble.

Yesterday my emotion was so unsure,
Today I am sure it's changing.
I shed a tear because I felt some fear,
Fear of what I am becoming,
What am I becoming?
I know.

Sure, positive, calm, I am now the one who can say no.
Enough is enough, I will take no more,
Because deep in the core of my heart
I know I am changing,
For the better, yes.
For the worse, no.
There is now a different me inside of me
And I am so glad I found it.

Gabrielle Cannon, Bury, Greater Manchester

SHADOWS

Shadows flickering on the wall,
How do they come to be there at all?
From the fire in the grate
Moving, shimmering till very late.
What do they do
These shifting shapes?
They dance on the wall
Like floating capes.
The fire dies down, it's very low
But still the shadows seem to know.
Their shapes are still there on the wall
But by now not quite so tall.

Muriel Clark, Brooklands, Greater Manchester

SUNDAY SOUL

Sunlight soaks the lichen-crusted wall,
Sparrows chatter in the creeper,
Pony clip-clops down Blackberry Lane,
Dreamy breeze softly lifts the curtain.
Old bells mellow pealing from the steeple
And in the chancel cool, diamond panes
Richly stained, light the hymns of the faithful.

The flat above the shop is drained of colour
Vacant windows splintered by the pounding.
Drugs and booze have flattened his soul
In a sea of indifference, lout is drowning.
Despises God and birds and flowers and trees
Could deride his mother, kill her
Kill himself or any other.

It's a lie that there's no devil and that youth is bliss.

Heather Ferrier, Failsworth, Greater Manchester

AUTUMN BREEZE

Russet shades of autumn are painted on the trees
Burnished bronze tinged yellow leaves rustle in the breeze
October breeze blows briskly, fluttering leaves float free
Sunlight shafts pierce shadows, lighting falling leaves

From which far country comes this breeze that cools the
shortening days?
And stirs the spirit as the leaves, now fallen, drift away
Its fingers bend the branches of the strong trees standing
tall
And dying leaves drift downwards as they heed the autumn
call

Joan M Jones, Prestwich, Greater Manchester

BABY ALEX

Alex is my cousin
A bouncing baby boy.

Nearly twelve months old
But still a bundle of joy.

He always has a smile for you
Morning, noon or night.

His eyes are like sunbeams
Always shining bright.

I love my cousin Alex
More than words can say.
One more thing I know for sure
My love for him grows more each day.

Emma Wilkinson, Salford, Greater Manchester

WHY

Why won't you tell me you love me
Before it's too late.
Why won't you tell me I'm needed
Before I walk through that gate.
Why won't you tell me there's something left
Worth saving for us to share.
Why won't you tell me I'm sometimes right
Or simply tell me that you still care.
Why if we've lost the love we once had
Why can't we try anew.
Why won't you let me prove to you
That I'm worth something too.

Connie Watson, Leigh, Greater Manchester

Born in Westhoughton, **Connie Watson** has interests including writing, swimming, art and walking. "When I retired I started putting down on paper my childhood memories about the war and my upbringing. Now I write about family and friends," she remarked. "My work is influenced by my fellow writers in the Leigh writers group and I would describe my style as very emotional, yet factual. I am a 71-year-old former singer with an ambition to be a versatile artist like Rolf Harris and an author like Jeffery Archer." Connie is married to Ron and they have six children.

MANCHESTER IN MAY

Flecks of white fall
Erratically around me.

Ash? Paper? Random rubbish?

Mirrored red cheeks,
My nose runs,
I sneeze.

This could be a biological attack,
I know this could happen,
I am in a big city
The government sent us a booklet.

A fleck touches my hand,
I flinch and wait
For my skin to start bubbling.

Then I relax as it melts and
My skin is enhanced by moisture,
Rather than ravaged by poison.

Manchester in May,
I didn't expect
Anything as innocent as snow.

Sarah Tucker, Manchester

GODS GARDEN

I have seen Gods garden,
It shimmers in the light.
The colours of the rainbow,
A pure and sheer delight.
Red roses bloom in splendour.
The orange lily grows
Yellow buttercups bedeck,
The emerald green meadow.
Blue forget me knots lead on
Where violets grow with pride.
And deep with each precious bloom,
A pure gold heart, sublime.

June Hellewell, Droylsden, Greater Manchester

BEAUTIFUL BEACH

As I pick up the warm sand
It just slips through my bare hand
On the beach, there is many a shell
An ice-cream van with lots to sell
We hear the loud, crashing waves
I love to explore the dark, rocky caves
Can we stay a while longer? I plead
So I may play amongst the seaweed
When I go and search for a crab
I think to myself, this beach is fab
I collected a shell and some rocks
Then hide them in a chest that locks
When I went fishing with my bucket and net
I tried to count the new people I'd met
For this exciting beautiful beach
Has many secrets to teach

Emily Beswick, Saddleworth, Greater Manchester

JOURNEY'S END

Today's the day
Journey's end
A new beginning
Straight ahead
Keep moving
Don't look back
The next step is now
The last one
A passed one
It will soon fall back
And join those which once were
And are now so far behind
Yet still part of the journey

Geoff Wilson, Chorlton, Greater Manchester

SLEEPY WOOD

Who knows the secret of Sleepy Wood,
In the dead of night when mortals lay
Their sleepy heads in deep slumber on their pillows,
They are not aware at all of what goes on deep in Sleepy
Wood.
Who is tolling the bluebells?
What is that strange and eerie cry?
And that chuckling, evil laughter,
Cascading through the night.
Should you hear the toll of the bluebells,
Pray do not go near.
For legend has it that mortals who dare, never reappear.
So stay where you are don't be tempted to leave,
For there is mischief afoot in the dead of night,
Deep in Sleepy Wood.

Mary Magilton, Oldham, Greater Manchester

TULIPS AND CHINESE NEW YEAR

Black women
Sitting on the floor
Around purple tulips
And flickering candles,
Chinese New Year
And Lin's birthday.
We celebrate
Our similarities,
Our differences,
Our double happiness.

Tina Tamsho-Thomas, Didsbury, Greater Manchester

Tina Tamsho-Thomas said: "I started creative writing when I was three and my work is influenced by cultural identity, nature and dreams. I am currently working on my autobiographical play *Dancin' in Sepia Dreams*, to be produced in 2006 and I am seeking a publisher for my children's story, *Yellow Bird Song*. I enjoy inspiring other writers by facilitating writing and performance workshops. My work has recently been published in *Brown Eyes*, a selection of creative expressions by black and mixed race women, edited by Nicole Moore. Other anthologies are available on request."

REALITY

What have I to dread? Is it death?
But Christ is my life, and I shall gain my death,
Is it banishment? But all the world and its fullness
Is the Lord's, is it loss of wealth?
But we brought nothing to this world and can carry
nothing out,
Thus all the terrors in the world are contemptible in my
eyes,
And I can only smile at its good things,
Poverty I do not dread,
Riches I do not desire,
From death I do not shrink,
And I desire life for so long as I can improve myself.
My wish is to have and to belong to someone,
To love and cherish for the rest of my life
Would be a worldly fulfilment and accomplishment.
Knowledge, I would like to have regarding all the events of
the world,
Its goodness, uncountable language capability,
To be able to understand not only humankind but also the
human mind,
With its different dialects and cultures,
Which includes their everyday life, going back to where
There was not so much complicated progress and
destruction.

Lilac Milton, Old Trafford, Greater Manchester

I SAW GOD IN THE CLOUDS LAST WEEKEND

I saw God in the clouds last weekend
This was the truth
I had not been seeking
As I reached for the final third of the bottle
Nothing too strong, not whisky
And not drinking to forget
Just an innocent bottle of red on a Saturday night

They say that searching too hard
Is not the way to the truth
But in a moment of happiness
Of carefree abandon
I saw God in the clouds last weekend
And I think he saw me

David Glover, Stockport, Greater Manchester

MESSAGE FROM THE MOON MAN

The man in the moon looked down on the land,
And thought to himself, isn't life grand.
Just sitting here in outer space,
With people gazing up at my face.

I'd best enjoy it while I can,
Before I'm over run by man.

Tramping all over and spoiling my face,
I can't help feeling it's a shocking disgrace.
Why they want to come, I'll never know,
There's nothing here, and nothing will grow.

No doubt they think they've been very clever,
But the mystery of the moon will have gone forever.

Jean Wood, Sale, Greater Manchester

BIRTH

A new life, a new beginning,
Strange how it makes you feel.

Seems only yesterday that you were born,
And now you have one of your own.

Our daughter has a daughter, we move on down the line,
A weird and wonderful passage is this thing called time.

As you hold out your child to us, we take her into our
hearts,
And this is where a family can again begin to start.

Lynne Goddard, Burnage, Greater Manchester

Dedicated to my beautiful grandaughter, Ruby.

TITANIC

The passengers
Rich and poor,
Their lives exist no more.
We all know of the ill fated journey,
Only fish admire your beauty at the bottom of the sea.
We all know what happened on that cold April night,
With just a small group of humans
Who saw the terrible sight.
Over fifteen hundred people did die,
Leaving their loved ones to weep and cry.
They said you were unsinkable,
Then you sank, did the unthinkable.
You lie on the seabed, all smelly and rotten,
But you are the ship, time will not have forgotten.

Thomas McGrath, Manchester

THE HAIRDRESSER

Are you sure she's alright under there?
Her face is getting redder,
And there's steam coming out of her ear holes
I think you'd better check her.

Are them curlers supposed to be smoking?
Is her hair meant to be flame red?
Is that really the look she wanted?
Are you sure that's what she said?

I think you should switch off the drier,
And check on what's left of her hair.
I think you should break it to her gently,
That there's really not a lot there!
Perhaps she'd like a new look?
Just tell her that blondes have more fun.
And show her the wig with the long golden locks,
Explain that the damage is done!

"My dear, what a transformation," as she walks out the
door
"I feel like I've got a new lease of life, I'll certainly come
back for more.
So you see, when life throws you troubles
It may end up for the good.
For she'd dreamt of looking like Bridget Bardot,
But never imagined she could!

Nikki Day, Sale, Greater Manchester

*Dedicated to all my wonderful friends who give me their time
and support unconditionally. Thank you.*

ELLEN MACARTHUR

Ellen what courage you have shown,
To voyage around the world.
In record time and all alone,
You succeeded. What a girl.

Seventy one days so many hours, to each second,
Breaking records previously set.
Your skill and stamina were all reckoned,
Remarkable Ellen, new record set.

You have been honoured as a dame,
Well done it's well-deserved.
For Ellen Macarthur you've made your name,
By showing all you had the nerve.

Margaret Ridgway, Rochdale, Greater Manchester

THE B OF THE BANG

Inspired by Linford, who begins to run
When the start of the race begins with the gun.
It's the b of the bang the race has begun
Sculpture for Manchester nearly reaching the sun.

We will remember the Commonwealth Games
The winners, the losers, what were their names?
It's huge and illuminated, what an impact
One hundred and eighty steel spikes, that's a fact.

"You can't please everybody," Heatherwick says
And a piece like this isn't made in days.
It's worth every penny of the one million.
Viewers and visitors will soon reach a billion.

Sylvia Lee-Wild, Rochdale, Greater Manchester

SHADOWS OF DARK SUBTERRANEAN LONELINESS

Shadows of dark subterranean loneliness
Alone and lost from your love above
She walks the earth while you retreat for the shelter
Blue skies and rain above
Darkness and oceans of tears below
Steps of chaos laughter and cries
Morning breaks amongst the lies - above
Steps of only me thinking of she
Longing for her light to shine on me - below
Wish she would fall through a passage to my soul
And light my torch
For my light will then forever shine
And my shadows of dark subterranean loneliness
Will then be dark and lonely without me

John Holmes, Liverpool, Merseyside

John Holmes said: "I have been writing poetry for about
seven years. I initially found it therapeutic to write about
personal experiences. When I realised this was poetic, my
writing phase began. I am a singer/songwriter and often
perform around Liverpool city centre, organising acoustic
based songwriter nights. I have a five year-old son who I
would love to teach guitar to when he is ready. I recently
graduated from Liverpool Community College with a HNC
Music Performance. I am a huge Bob Dylan fan and I think
he is a fabulous poet and songwriter. I hope readers of
poetry will share in my personal expression and enjoy my
poem."

I SEE LIGHTS

Run down buildings, broken smile
Twenty pence or next door's child?
People stare and people cry
No-one taught me how to fly.

Trapped memories in the hall of your birth
Look back on life, assess its worth.
The love you had turns to frantic glance
All we ever did was dance.

The ones you love are the ones who burn,
No time to see, no time to learn.
Cut up photos, vacant eyes,
Build your canvas, paint with lies.

It is nobler to never get paid
Than to profit from tears and dismay
Cheap cafes and bargain flights
Some see darkness, I see lights.

Tom Gorton, Heswall, Merseyside

AUTUMN AND SPRING

I'm nearing autumn you are still spring,
I only meant this to be a fling.
But it goes deeper than I thought,
Into my life such joy you have brought.

An Adonis who says he loves me,
Deep down inside I know it can't be.
You promise that you will always be true,
I don't know what I'll do without you.

You'll break my heart when you go away,
And I'm not sure how I'll face that day.
You've given me more than you know,
But I'll survive when you have to go.

Don't let it be yet, stay for a while,
You are the one who can make me smile.
If I were younger we'd have a chance,
But I know soon we'll have our last dance.

Ann Blair, Prenton, Merseyside

ECHOES

You say: soft things prevent sound penetration.
Is it silent at the centre of the Earth?
 Do soft things protect us from surface noises?
What is the mystery behind burial rites?
 Do layers cause spatial deflection or do they absorb?
Is the return to Earth an ageing archetype which elephants
remember?
 Does this coat stop others hearing my heart beat?
What is silence? The death of sound
 How can this room stop solid thoughts sounding?
What is sound? The death of silence
 If a soft body absorbs sound, does it there remain?
Surely then, death is but the suspension of echoes
resounding...

Barbara Murray, Liverpool, Merseyside

HIGH ANXIETY

He was filled with great anxiety
Time was rushing by
How would he able to cope?
With it all
He was really afraid to fly
Should he just pretend he was not bothered
Nonchalantly walk on the plane
Or get smashed beforehand, he would never do this again
He became very talkative
Jabbering on and on, I've had quite enough of this
Behaving like his young son
Get a grip of yourself, I say
You are supposed to set an example
We're not flying till December
It's only February the fifth today

Maureen Holt, Kirkby, Merseyside

HAIKU IN PARIS

Paris by moonlight
Dining in style to music
On the bateau mouche

Under the bridges
Reflections in the water
Lantern's golden light

Music, sweet and low
Enchanted by the harpist
Waist length silken hair

Japanese tourists
Young, charming and innocent
Break into a song

Low, sad and gentle
A beautiful melody
Strangely touches me
With shameful regret
I recall the sheer horror
Of Hiroshima

Don McLean, Irby, Merseyside

Don McLean said: "I qualified as a Chartered Engineer, and worked in engineering management until retirement. Whilst youngsters, my two children used to appreciate my bedtime stories. Years later, I took an OU arts degree. My interest in creative writing was further stimulated through part-time University extension courses. In 2003, I became a full time student at the University of Liverpool and was awarded an MA in Science Fiction. I have been involved in the amateur theatre for many years, but have given up acting and directing for a return to storytelling - this time in print."

HE WHO WAITS

Have patience child
Everything comes to he who waits.
Dreams run wild
It is never too late.

Everything comes to he who waits
But not too soon.
Never too late
A trip to the moon.

A small step for man
A giant step for mankind.
Enjoy it while you can
But have patience child.

Everything comes to he who waits
Heaven is what we wait for.
Open up them pearly gates
And give me more, more, more.

Antony Haselton, Newton-le-Willows, Merseyside

MY THOUGHTS

To be desperate and lonely
But to be at home with the family.
I know what it's like.

To hear that murderous scream from within
That is silent to the world.
I know what it's like.

To feel the frustration, the will to do everything
But the situation not available.
I know what it's like.

The life that is your one and only chance
That is slipping by so quickly.
I know what it's like.

The only freedom to look forward to
Is the peaceful release in death.
I am waiting to know what it's like.

Ruth Goldsworthy, Tranmere, Merseyside

APPETITE

I can't take it
I complain for the fifth time this week,
Adverts for a better life and ice white bright teeth
All manor of plastic carrots and the politics of fear
All manor of consumer goods, for now, for how, for here
And while I'm looking for something to quell my hunger
I'm blinded by the media designed to make me wonder
I stumble, I falter, I linger
I purchase their dreams and still I hunger
This appetite damning me quietly,
Petitioning so insidiously
Questioning just what it is I can buy me
To satiate this spiral of hypnotic necessity

S L P-Adams, Prenton, Merseyside

THE CREAM OF LOVE

The cream of love is vividly not pugnacious,
Nevertheless judicious.
One welcomes the cream with promptness.
Henceforth I will feel nothing but joy,
Neurotic no more,
Don't find life a bore,
Glad, not sad.

The cream of love one finds
If not inexplicable.
I give it utter approbation.
Life's soothing,
Full of so much merriment,
Content one has got the true
Cream of adoration, veneration.

D Doyle, Waterloo, Merseyside

SUNDAY WORSHIP

I no longer go to church any more
But instead give my motor a wash.
Good bye to the candle the bell and the book
And hello to the bucket and splosh.

I worship my car and it carries me far
Though the petrol is very expensive,
I can drive to the shops or some funky night spots
The list of the trips is extensive.

When I'm driving along I sing an old song
And remember my days without wheels,
The improvement is such with the gears and the clutch
I can show you a clean pair of heels.

Francis Hogan, Barnston, Merseyside

Francis Hogan said; "I have been writing poems and articles over the past 12 years and receiving advice and criticism from my local writers' group, Wirral Writers. I have been married for 39 years and have two married daughters. My favourite poems are Kipling's Banack Room Ballads."

AUTUMN'S GOLDEN CARPET

Rusty shades of orange and gold,
Reds and yellows to behold.
Leaves abandon to the ground,
No finer vista to be found.
Winds are blowing, swirling round,
Swarming leaves impact the ground.

Lingering at first, then in speed,
Rushing down, it was their need.
Like a waterfall tumbling down,
Forever spinning to the ground.
A thousand leaves forever dropping,
Cascading leaves never stopping.

As the leaves keep falling deep,
This was autumn's golden sleep.
Trees laid bare with buds exposed,
Revealed, uncovered and disclosed.
Held in wait, seals autumn's fate,
While winter's lingering at the gate.

Isobel Cullen, Prenton, Merseyside

LIGHTHOUSE

A tall, slim column holding a light,
Which beams out its fire into the night.
The spray of the surf and rocks far below,
In the revolving light, they appear to glow.
The creaking mast of an old ship,
Heaving and pitching, her wheel starts to slip.

As mountainous waves crash on the deck,
The spray and salt water stream down the neck.
While sailors battle to keep the huge ship on course,
The sea and wind building to storm force.
With the ship's crew battling the swell and the spray,
The oil lamps are blazing, they rock and sway.

The roll of the ship, makes it hard to stand,
While black, jagged rocks jut out from the land.
The rigging soaking as men start to climb,
Out on the spars, one at a time.
Pulling in sail that they call a sheet,
Gripping the rigging in wet, bare feet.

Brian Williams, Southport, Merseyside

MOTHERS

They tuck you up and kiss you goodnight,
And when they turn out the light,
They sit with you until you're alright.

They hug you when you scrape your knees,
And worry when you're climbing trees.
And even though you fight and bawl,
You love each other after all.

Your mum is your best friend and stands by you,
No matter what you're going through.
After all, they think about you every day,
And care for you in every way.

Heather McCavish, Wallasey, Merseyside

WHAT IS PERFECTION?

Is perfection to hold the world in your hand?
To have power and money,
To look important and grand.

Is it to be an overachiever, with an academic mind?
To be knowledgeable and clever,
But also considerate and kind.

Is it all about looks that people envy you constantly?
Or is it about books?
For you to be shrewd, yet still sophisticated,

So when you look in the mirror,
Do you see perfection?
I just see me,
A humble reflection.

Lauren Gould, Bromborough, Merseyside

A WINTER'S NIGHT

The road rolled out like a bracelet
Into the velvet night
The wet road looked like gold
Reflecting the coloured street light

One side of the road were rubies
Lights of receding cars
The oncoming cars were diamonds
Twinkling like the stars

In the distances shone an emerald
Shining through the rain
It changed to an amber, then ruby
Then back to emerald again

I drove down this bracelet and pondered
As I gazed around at the sight
There's beauty around for seeing
Even on a cold, wet winter's night

Jean Beasor, Moreton, Merseyside

Jean Beasor said: "I have been making up verse for as long as I can remember but only started writing it down when I took a creative writing course two years ago. I am a widow with three children and seven grandchildren. I enjoy hill-walking, gardening and foreign holidays. I am writing my life story so that my grandchildren and future generations will know what life was like for a child living in the country in the 1940s."

LOVE IS...

Love is happiness
Love is kindness
Love is love
Love is one big family
Love is sharing
Love is caring
Love is looking after each other
Love is thinking of others before yourself
Love is being there for each other
Love is gods way for us to follow him
Love is giving each other your things
Love is looking out for each other
Love is god's family
Love is blue
Love is from the heart
Love is not a joke
Love is being nice to each other
Love is helping each other
Love is something you cannot see
Love is a mystery

Emily Ablett, Newton-le-Willows, Merseyside

AT WARWICK CASTLE

Distantly I hear the plaintive cry
That tinged the summer air with sadness.
Down the shorn and shaven green,
The great bird strode.
A miniature galleon, sailing
The tropical waters of his own plumage.
Iridescent against the grey walls,
He strutted, head aloft,
Plumed coronet quivering.

I sat bewitched by his presence,
A half-eaten sandwich poised.
Then he lurched clumsily, half-hop,
Half-flight, comical in his greed,
Onto the back of my seat.
Pecking like a God come down to earth
To eat with mortals.
I smiled, watching his gold rimmed eye
Searching for crumbs,
And loved him more.

Georgina Southern, Wallasey, Merseyside

AN ABSENT FRIEND

His home was humble, little money had he,
Whatever he had, Ben shared with me.
Enjoying together a simple meal, lovingly prepared,
He showing, each knowing, how much he cared.
Long walks we took together each day,
Whether skies were sunny or grey.
Sometimes ambling along deserted shore,
Stopping to listen to distant ocean roar.
Hours spent tramping through a nearby wood,
Between us a silence which both understood.
Winter evenings just sitting, quietly content,
Two great companions, their energies spent.
The house now is silent, without his familiar feet
Relatives whisper, as they leave, they weep.
Ben, my faithful friend was buried today,
In a black hearse, under flowers he lay.
Never were two so lovingly bound,
Old Ben, aged master, me his hound.
For a dog never had so true a friend,
Now sadly I wait for my journey to end.

K Moyses, Southport, Merseyside

HEART OF THE RIVER

My people,
Encompassed in the articulation of an azul
Perfection,
Living terrain; refusal of slumber,
Snowball engraved to jade herbs,
Ripples of past debt to act, ack ack dreams,
Callous deaceasement, threads of circumference,
Rain of adoration,
Veil of reposed light returning to embracement,
Yielding each soul to lodge cures,
Scarlet doves, condoning emulation of soft yielded
Kisses, culture of diplomatic
Beautiful pulse of the river.

Rachel Cromwell, Liverpool, Merseyside

PEN?

A simple pen is fine
For when you spend half your time
Writing and doodling
Scribbling and caboodling
You notice that it's the simple things
That can inspire
Enlighten
Give your imagination wings

Carve mountains with your imagery
An intellectual filigree
Twisting spirals to make you think
A new dimension cast in ink
This simple pen is the life line link
The path meandering to the brink
Of the cliff's coast lining my mind

Elizabeth Gill, Meols, Merseyside

A DARK SNOWY MORNING

My world was black white and blue
There was such a to do
The white snow was very deep
It all happened while I was asleep

The shadows were a beautiful blue
Thrown by the hedges across the lane
The footprints of the postman too
Natures playing a different game

The trees are bare black against the sky
Unheeding of you or I
When evening comes the feelings change
The blackness creeps along the lane

The lantern swings the shadows move
It's scary now the sky is dark
There is no moon or stars to shine
My world is black no white or blue
Does it feel like that to you

Vera Tague, Liverpool, Merseyside

Vera Tague said: "I am 68. When my five children were small I used to tell them stories each evening before I took them to bed, but at that time I never thought of writing them down. Last year, I joined a creative writing class in the Rotunda Community College where I receive plenty of encouragement from the tutor and students. Many of my ideas come from the long walks I take in the countryside surrounding the city of Liverpool. My other hobby is oil painting. I find that this helps me to see what is there and to put down in words what my hands try to put down with paint."

GHOSTS

They can sneak up suddenly behind you
And whisper in your ear
And glide within your line of vision
Sometimes far and sometimes near
And all the time they're shadowy
Not as solid looking as a living person would appear
Though their voices whisper loudly
And their words are true and meaningfully clear
For they carry all times in their tones
And they come to say important things and to be seen
That disturbs us in our world
For we believe a distance lies between
Their ghostly realm and ours
That converge as we live our life;
But one day we will understand as yet
That ghosts are necessary to give of good advice.
But one day we will understand
As we glide as ghosts around the stars
That we have become the same as them;
The spirits humans see on earth and try to disregard.

Christine Hale, Wallasey, Merseyside

EACH DAY

Evening sunshine on wet sand
Lovers walking hand in hand
A rugged shoreline by the calm sea
A pretty picture you will agree
A fishing village, very quaint
Rows of houses that need a lick of paint
Cafés and boutiques which thrive
During summer, when tourists arrive
Cobble stones, well weathered
Gypsy horses on grass edges tethered
Chiming church bells on Sunday
Local people on their way
Bumblebees and butterflies in flight
Really are a super sight
The smell of lilies with their heady scent
Roses, of course, so elegant
Chrysanthemums tall and straight
Growing by the garden gate
Make every day a memory
And happy you will always be

Heather Cattle, Southport, Merseyside

THE UNKNOWN

When we say that love will never die,
That we will love forever,
What happens when we die?

Does that love live on like some gentle breeze,
That slowly rises in the sky
And waits there for a lover's tryst?

How can we know,
We mean it when we say that we
Will always love each other,
Or will that end like memories
In the mist of time?

H Kenny, Crosby, Merseyside

MY SOUL'S WAKE

Years ago in deprived quarter one
Further back with so much energy
Spirit visible and no plans to runaway
Further on with just physical entity, just tangible
Something you can see
Something's not right with me
All old spirit's gone
All my soul has flown
I watch and sob for my wake
I live in mourning and pray for a new soul
The old soul's a long time dead
It's not about reincarnation nor life after death
It's deserted me and the hurt's gone to my head
All those words return from their graves
"You cannot leave me yet, there are things to do here"
I've waited for a reply since the sombre funeral
I'm desperate for a meaning, a certified meaning

Andy Powell, Liverpool, Merseyside

AN AUTUMN RAMBLE

Beneath the trees, the dying leaves,
Consumed by worms and lowly things,
Lie trampled in the autumn earth,
Where hides the seeds of coming spring,
And badgers rummage through the grass,
Awaiting summer's warmth at last.

Upon the branch a robin stands,
And puffs his breast against the cold,
While families with cheerful stride,
The wonders of the woods behold,
To gaze in awe at nature's might,
While squirrels hurry out of sight.

Such loveliness in green and brown,
The eyes of mankind to admire,
The beauty of the rolling hills,
To kindle passion's warming fire,
What love our Father God has shown,
To make these things for us alone.

Tony Tasak, Prenton, Merseyside

Tony Tasak said: "As a Christian, I try to glorify God in all
that I do. On weekends I may be found at fairs, re-enact-
ments, or on the streets of Chester dressed in Tudor attire
singing and playing an early guitar, proclaiming the Gospel
and handing out sonnets telling of the good news of
Salvation. I also compose epithalamia and can perform at
weddings, garden parties etc. See www.craftyminstrel.com
for further information."

THE ANSWER

The answer sometimes lies in the flickering coals,
The leaves in your tea cup or the curtain as it folds.
The answer can be found in the leaves on the ground,
It is there to be found if you look around.

Your future was patterned before you were born,
So don't give up hope if you're feeling all torn.
Tomorrow is always another day
And better things could be coming your way.

"Good times equal bad" it's a saying that's true.
It applies to all beings, not just me or just you.

So don't feel alone in this world full of hate,
Good times are ahead, you may just have to wait.

Look around, look around, the answer is there.
Maybe somebody else wants your problem to share.
Someone who'll love you, someone who'll care.
Look around, look around, the answer is there!

Joyce Loftus, Moreton, Merseyside

LETTING GO

I, strung tight as a bow,
You, straight and true as an arrow.
I will release you.
You will climb and fly
As you catch the wind.
"Where to?" say you
"Anywhere," say I,
The sky is no limit.
And if you fall,
I will be there
To pick you up
And send you on your way.
I will never falter
In my quest to keep you flying.
I am your bow, you are my arrow,
Each needing the other,
For you are my child and I am your mother.

Janet Hughes, Southport, Merseyside

*Dedicated to my daughters Vicky, Kathy, Tracey and Mandy
and all my future generations.*

HAUNTED

Darkness all around her
She finds it harder and harder to breathe
As the memories weigh hard on her fragile heart
A tear rolls down her cheek.

They tear at her clothes and she tears out her hair
She screams but it falls on deaf ears
They gnaw at her arms until they are gaping and raw
And her blood eats it's way through her sheets.

She puts up a fight, such a brave little soul
But illusion will tear her apart
The fragments of broken existence
Pierce her heart every night as she sleeps.

Viki Duffy, Wavertree, Merseyside

CROUCH COTTAGE

Does anyone live in this cottage,
With windows webbed and grimed,
Where filigree snail trails pattern the walls,
In slithery, silvery slime?

Listen.
The leaves in restless mounds,
Mutter beside the door,
Lift and drift round the chimney pot,
Then pirouette to the floor.

I'll peer inside through the murky glass.
The twilit, shrouded room,
Seems to be waiting on tip-toe,
For a witch to return on her broom.

Shirley Tomlinson, Formby, Merseyside

END OF THE DAY

I lay in bed listening to the rain,
Gently tapping on every pane.
The wind whistled, in the night sky,
Angry at the noise of a plane going by.
The drone of its engines, gave me a fright,
I stared at it, till it went out of sight.
The trees in the garden, bent with the breeze,
Once more I lay there, feeling at ease.
My mind was drifting, to times in the past,
I yawned, ah well, sleep is coming at last.
Turning over to face the wall,
Feeling contented, I whispered, goodnight all.

Harry Shaw, Crosby, Merseyside

Born in Liverpool, **Harry Shaw** has interests including writing, crosswords and eating out. "I first started writing poetry in 1984, and resumed it again last year after being given a computer," he pointed out. "My work is influenced by anything I find funny or sad, and I would describe my style as easy-going, sincere and sentimental. I would like to be remembered as someone who had a great sense of humour and was loyal, loving, sincere and honest." Aged 68, Harry is a retired driver with an ambition to have more of his work published. He is a widower with three sons.

THE BIRDS OF THE AIR

The birds of the air, they fly so high
Up above the sky
They swoop and dive and fly so freely
It must be a lovely feeling to have that freedom too
Just think what I could do

Even the humble sparrow
Darts and flies away
The babies in their nest are taught to fly
As soon as they leave their mother's side

The cocky robin struts around
Looking for food on the ground
But flees from thieving magpies when they appear
Oh dear, oh dear

I sometimes envy the birds of the air
Because I can only stand and stare
How I wish that I was there
Oh dear, oh dear

P McDowell, Liverpool, Merseyside

THE OLD TRUNK

My dad's old tin trunk that he took to sea
It was orangey brown
With lots of things inside
There was a piece of an old wireless
The cover of an old violin solo by Coleridge Taylor
A bit of old newspaper
With adverts for ladies' coats and the price of old slippers
Doc Dan's this and that
A rub of this would cure all that ills you
It also had a bible with a pretty picture of Samuel as he
heard God's voice
He was looking up to see the Heavens
There was Bubbles with his lovely curly hair
A picture of two birds singing in a birdcage
One little slipper
It had belonged to a baby who had died long ago
I close the lid on the old tin box
My memories are safe
My dad's old violin book
The smell of the sea
Bring old memories back to me

Mary Barnes, Liverpool, Merseyside

BATS

I am a bat,
My wings slicing through the air,
As I fly so high,
Through the wonderful, calm night sky.

Through the darkness I travel,
Sneaky as can be,
As I fly so high so high,
Through the wonderful, warm night sky.

Hovering past the glowing moon,
You know I'm a bat,
As I fly so high,
Through the wonderful, peaceful night sky.

Charlotte Hughes, Woodchurch, Merseyside

WHO AM I?

Snake-like eyes glisten,
Softly in the pale moonlight,
The gentle splash of my quarry,
Quiet or it might take flight.
My powerful muscles move me,
Slowly, creeping closer, taking my time,
The dear, she cannot see me,
Tonight I'll make her mine.
I lower myself cautiously, to start the final assault,
Leaving just my eyes and nose on show.
She senses the tension and prepares to bolt,
A lunge, a snap, alas for poor Jane Doe,
Her nature meek and mild,
But she was no match for little old me,
An alligator truly wild.

Kathrine Taylor, Bootle, Merseyside

WE'LL ALWAYS LOVE YOU

Always waiting, hoping soon to hear the key in the lock,
Listening when all that you hear is the sound of the clock,
Oh how I wish our Michelle was in her bed safe and sound,
But in her bedroom now there's emptiness all around,
She's grown up now, a mind of her own, she's nineteen
years old
Oh, how one tries to guide her into some kind of mould,
Yet in your heart you know that she is still a child,
Grown up in some ways, but can still be stubborn and
wild,
We'll always love you Michelle, we'll always be here for you,
Your mum and dad watched over you as slowly you grew,
Into now what you are, a beautiful daughter so dear,
And in our hearts you know, you will always be held near.

Elsie Prenton, Liverpool, Merseyside

Born in Liverpool, **Elsie Prenton** has interests including
poetry, reading and making cards. "I was encouraged to
write poetry by my mother when I was very young," she
pointed out. "My work is also influenced by my life experiences and I would like to be remembered as a kind and
caring person who looked after her family." Aged 61, Elsie
is retired and has ambitions to continue writing poetry and
have more of her work published. She is married to George
and they have one daughter. "My biggest fantasy is to be
pampered aboard a cruise liner and my worst nightmare is
drowning," she added.

SMALL TREMORS

Twelve fifty-six am, September, Sunday, small hours,
The earth moved suddenly,
The room trembled about us,
But we passed it off as something else.
Earthquakes don't happen in England,
And believing isn't easy these days.

Answers are often uninspiring,
Questions should always be interesting,
Even when our world is rocked,
And we're dazed within the aftershock.
We turn on the news and pay attention
To a stranger talking form the epicentre.

So absorbed in separate isolation,
Everyone making sounds of communication
And saying nothing but clichés
That patronise, eventually immunise
Us against original lust and temptation,
Even earthquakes don't rock our world.

Paula Morris, Wallasey, Merseyside

SYCAMORE

Twin-trunked sycamore
Sun sifting.
Each leafy gesture held
By branches that know
The convolutions of
Self and neighbour.

Arms as old as England
Carrying the family face
This leafy mosaic miracle
Each in its proper place.

No two trees twinned
Yet all are sycamore
What is this sycamore-ness
That courses through their veins?

And what is it that my smaller frame
For nature, is conveying?
Are we all incandescent carriers
Of her eternal flame?

Nick Buchanan, Wallasey, Merseyside

THE LEGACY

Children - dally no more upon veiled ground,
Lest you forsake what one cannot glean.
Surly terrain may well vent its spleen
Where dormant sentinel soldiers abound
Follow not the farmer, who tills the earth,
Where scattered sterile seeds still remain.
Abandoned by a conflict condemned insane
Which brought widespread death and dearth.
Who will rid the world of this ugly blemish?
Eradicate the peril from a blighted land.
Will succour weave its patterned strand?
When nations postulate the many premise.
Why must man resort to this hideous course?
When clearly he's astride wars apocalyptic horse.

William Carr, Liverpool, Merseyside

THE HAND OF A FRIEND

In my days of dark despair,
You were the friend who was always there.
You believed in me when I lost my way,
You listened and helped me through each day.
I was weak but you were strong,
It was your faith in me that helped me along.
There aren't many friends on earth like you,
Who gave me the courage to see things through.
I felt a failure on the road to despair,
But you held out your hand,
You were always there.
When I made it through hell's dark tunnel,
To the bright, shining light at the end,
You were there to praise me,
My dear and only friend.

Lydia Bowdidge, Prenton, Merseyside

HANDS

Hands are flexible and stretchable,
They're beautiful but breakable.
Inside-out and outside-in,
All encased in glove-like skin.
Like a sampler carefully sewn,
Sinews, tendons, skin and bone.
Flowing streams of brightest red,
Cushioned in veins on floating bed.
Pianist's hands, supple, spreadable,
Babies hands, so small, incredible.
Our hands are used each day from birth,
There is no price to state their worth.

Barbara Nuttall, Spital, Merseyside

Dedicated to the fracture and orthopaedic clinic at Arrowe Park Hospital, Wirral.

Born in the Wirral, **Barbara Nuttall** has interests including watercolours, crown green bowling and china painting. "I started writing poetry at school and my work is influenced by life itself. I would describe my style as true and sincere, and I would like to be remembered for my sense of humour," explained Barbara. Aged 67, she is retired and has an ambition to write much more poetry. She is married to Eric and has one daughter and two stepsons. "The person I would most like to be for the day is Victoria Wood and I would love to meet Pam Ayres because I like her poems and humour," added Barbara.

SUNDAY MORNING

Over the garden a stillness hangs.
Curtains closed.
A cat creeps stealthily along a fence top
Returning from his nightly roaming.
The dawn chorus, now over,
Is busy, feeding, flying.

No traffic heard, roads deserted.
Houses full of people, yet unseen.
Slumbering away their week's work
In the knowledge of a day not measured by time.
No alarm clock set, except the children.

The gardens, open to the elements
Can tell a tale of the previous evening.
They whisper the nocturnal doings
Of snails, hedgehogs, bats and cats.

All the sleepiness is rubbed away
By the opening of curtains
And packets of bacon.

Sue Farley, Knotty Ash, Merseyside

HOUSE OF CARDS

Angelic voice is heard by choice,
Through fellow cupids lost in rhyme.
The King of Hearts, with heart its parts,
Wishes dearly she were mine.
Between my self and the stage,
A war we wage mounts agonising distress,
For need of but a guess to remedy this mess,
As a result, I pay no heed.

The joker of the pack beside myself
Also viewing the angel, but in different light.
The smoke-screen his sight penetrates,
As admired by myself,
Clouds his judgement to which he proved
Swaying my queen of diamonds,
Shattering her tower to the ground.

Love, shared by all but desired by the weak,
Want for the ideal target of which we all seek,
But never found for lust for the better,
Or insecurities of the past.
Lives directed by fifty-two variables
And inspired by the cast.

James A Sambrooks, Liverpool, Merseyside

THREE HUNDRED AND FORTY FIVE
WHO WANTS TO BE AN ADULT

Who wants to be an adult
And go to work all day
No more fun and laughter
No more games or play

Who wants to be an adult
With the responsibility it entails
Dressing up all fancy
No more trainers or pigtails

The whole world is about money
The older that you get
Life is no longer happy
It's sad filled with regret

So who wants to be an adult
Certainly not me
I don't want the worries and woes
I just want to be free

Sarah Louise Carroll, Liverpool, Merseyside

Dedicated to my mum, my nan and my grandads Francis and Billy.

TIMELESS

Brown clock
Stopped.
Hands point to midnight,
Movement gone.

Sitting in its favoured
Place,
Gravely surveys,
Space before face.

Liquid?
Static?
Solid?
A galaxy without form?

Sybil Willcox, Liverpool, Merseyside

GETTING RINSED

One cigarette,
One glass of wine,
Might help me ease my state of mind.

Make it another,
What harm can it do?
It may help myself get over you.

Oh help, I've downed the bottle.
I don't feel much better,
I'm still alone now,
And I've been sick on your sweater.

Lauren Brooks, West Kirby, Merseyside

Dedicated to all that 141 Mansfield Road was.

AGNOSTIC PRAYER

Show me what you know is best,
Tomorrow will do.
Shed a light upon my quest
And clarify the view.

Give my reason chance to rhyme,
Keep me hopeful for mankind.
Send me sight behind my eyes
Of what I fail to realise,
That only with a growth in time,
Will answers sprout
And reason rhyme.

Robert Warwick Green, Wallasey, Merseyside

Dedicated to my daughter Jessica Joy, without whom my world would be a shallow grave indeed. Thanks for your smile.

Born in Scotland, **Robert Warwick Green** has interests including fishing and taxidermy. "I started composing poetry in 1979 after a long illness, and I do not let anyone or anything influence my work," he explained. "I would describe my style as contemporary realism and I would like to be remembered with affection and respect." Aged 55, Robert works as a carpenter and has an ambition to have all his written work in print for others to enjoy. "The person I would most like to see is my mother who is 88 and lives in New Zealand," added Robert.

ANOTHER RAINY DAY

The skies are grey
Everywhere is dull
Nobody's out
Everybody's bored
And I can't stand it anymore
I can't take it anymore

Another rainy day, the skies are grey
And the ground is wet like the sea
I see the rain falling down on me

I see you look at the
Dull grey sky
Oh how I wish it
Would go away
Come back
Some other day
And I can't take it anymore
I can't stand it anymore

Another rainy day, the skies are grey
And the ground is wet like the sea
I see the rain falling down on me

Shaun Daly, Birkenhead, Merseyside

JOURNEY TO THE SEA

Snow capped mountains cold and bleak,
Much too high for goats and sheep,
Await the spring, the expected thaw
When down to the valley the melt will pour.
As rills, runnels and rivulets cascade,
Not stopped by dams, dykes or barricade.

Cold water enters the valley stream,
Enlivening the trout of the angler's dream.
Meandering along the gorse and heather
Tinkling and bubbling, light as a feather.

Along the miles of lush green meadow
To enter the river where oarsmen row.
The water here is slow and deep
Beneath its mud, bream, tench and carp do sleep.

The water looks so slow and cold,
But the volume's increased a thousand fold.
Down to its estuary on a circuitous route
Over the tidal pan like muddy soup.
In a myriad of channels the water hides
Then all do varnish in the incoming tides.

D F Jones, Moreton, Merseyside

TIME SLIP

Standing on the quayside
Watching the fog swirl round
A sailing ship appears
Its horn the only sound
Ghostly figures on the deck
Search the murky mist
Host the skull and crossbones
There's another ship
Cannons roll, the captain shouts
Pistols and cutlasses ready
Then they go and sail right through
The Liverpool to Seacombe ferry

John Mutton, Liverpool, Merseyside

WHAT I AM

Here I am,
Floating over the edge,
One step between
Life and death.
Should I fall?
Should I go against the force that pulls so strongly?
Should I be scattered to the wind
With my fears
Carefree and calm?
I leap into the breeze.
Let it carry me to a better place,
Let me be one with life.
I've been waiting for this moment.
I plummet down,
Down,
Elated,
I am the wind.

Amanda Dodd, Birkenhead, Merseyside

SLIP INTO TYRANNY

We get complacent with all we have
We think in forevers
That it will all last
But waiting is tyranny
That we have no sight to see
No stomach to tense
And no mindset to fight.

The sceptre of apathy has silenced us
Our voice has been stifled by inaction
Baleful bonds in the form of words
Cascade from a crooked mind spilled onto paper and
stapled together
A constitution of forfeited rights is born

We look at the past and laugh
"Never again" and "Can't happen, not to us"
But unguarded, unchecked we will all become slaves again.

Stephen Thelwell, St Helens, Merseyside

Born in Whiston, **Stephen Thelwell** has interests including
writing, reading and sport. "I started writing poetry when I
was a teenager to let out anger and fight depression," he
explained. "My work is influenced by black metal music
and politics, and I would describe my style as a mix of horror, anger and sadness." Aged 24, Stephen has an ambition
to become a great lyricist. "I have written radio and stage
plays as well as around 200 poems, and my biggest fantasy
is to be a guitarist in a metal band," he added.

HEROES

They marched with such great dignity, proudly, heads held
high
The debt we owe to these brave men no-one can deny.
Their courage and bravery can still be seen today
No-one knows the horrors they faced, nor the price they
had to pay,
Gallantly running forward into no-mans land
Across smoke-filled sodden terrain,
Bayonets fixed in their hands.
Mud-filled trenches, stale canned food, chaos all round
Comrades dying, gunfire blasting but,
They still stood their ground.
Vivid memories they still recall, those days of living hell
Because of all they went through, they alone can tell.
The suffering and the nightmares they still relive each day
The many friends they made and lost, as though it were
yesterday.
Returning home as heroes, those men who were so brave
Those who never made it home lay in foreign graves.
Millions of white marble gravestones
Gleaming in the sun.
Lay someone's precious loved ones
Husbands, fathers, sons.

Mary Murray, Bootle, Merseyside

ROYAL AND ANCIENTS

There they stand, sentinels in the mist
Shrouded by mystery, shaped yet shapeless
White, crystallised, fragile yet not

Guardians of the countryside, aged yet timeless
Overseeing man and his tamperings
Working with the seasons to keep nature alive

Slowly the sun rises, warms the freezing winter air
Slowly the mist vanishes, leaving substance, solidity
Still in majesty they stand

How tall they appear, spreading arms reaching out
No clothes yet warm and warming all around
No colour but so many shades and hues

Faces gnarled and skin multi-wrinkled
Limbs, bent, curled, twisted and stretching
Reaching out with arthritic-like hands

Regal, almost God-like, within their surroundings
These ancients who provide shelter, food and rest
They will be when we are long gone
These grand English oaks

M T Daly, Birkenhead, Merseyside

YESTERYEARS

Store up your memories
Pack them away
One day when you're older they'll brighten your day
The tiny scent bottle your son won for you
A page from a school book, your daughter's first shoe
The love of your mother
Your father's cigar
A posy of daisies from a boy you admired
The smile on the face of a loving grandchild
And married contentment just sat by the fire
So when I feel lonely I just close my eyes
And draw on my memories of such happy times.

Jean Beattie, Liverpool, Merseyside

JUST ME

The monster in my hand
Pushed little Harry off his chair
Tugged dumpy Susie's bright red hair
It was the monster that did this, you see
Nothing to do with me.

There was a monster in my leg
Kicked skinny Jimmy to the floor
He was frightened of me, so he got more
The monster did this you see
Nothing to do with me.

There were monsters in my head
I am older now, feel sad, shame
Nothing, no-one else to blame
Why, long ago, could I not see?
There are no monsters, just me.

Ans Dodd Prins, Crosby, Merseyside

153

TOMMY'S FAREWELL

Please don't send me away mam
I promise I'll be good.
Don't want to go with our Jimmy
And I'll miss your suet pud.
You and dad say we'll be safe in another land
Away from fires and bombing.
But I'll miss holding your hand
I don't know how to wear my gas mask.
Or properly tie my laces
Our Jimmy keeps telling me off,
Because I can't keep up with his paces.
I can hear the steam train coming
I know I mustn't cry.
But I can't stop the tears falling
No matter how hard I try.
I'm trying to be brave
Be strong in every situation.
Trouble is mam I don't understand
What is evacuation?

Polly Pawson, Birkenhead, Merseyside

Born in Birkenhead, **Polly Pawson** has interests including writing, reading, gym training and dancing. "I started writing poetry in my school days and my work is influenced by comic situations, making new friends and my life in the Wirral," she explained. "I would describe my style as varied but mainly humorous and I would like to be remembered as a lovable poet, mother and grandmother." Polly is married to Tony and has six children. "I am currently writing a book about my life and also a children's book, and I have written over 100 poems," she added.

A BABY'S EYES

What is the hidden secret when I gaze into the eyes?
The wonder of this, my first born grandchild
A reflection of the past as memories unfold
Things long forgotten come back so bold

Memories of my firstborn locked deep inside
That feeling of elation, a bursting of pride
Nothing can equal that feeling within
As I look in wonder at my grand daughter's eyes

A precious little package entrusted to us
So small and helpless with a need to be loved
Days so short with long, sleepless nights
But every one worth it for this little mite

No-one can say how a gift so small
Can bring so much feeling and love to us all
The wonder of nature that's locked deep inside
Comes out in us all, through a new baby's eyes

So my dear daughter, I'll say this to you
Enjoy your daughter the way I've enjoyed you
There's no greater feeling than that of the pride
Unlocked to us now through your baby's eyes

J I Sherlock, Moreton, Merseyside

WINTER

Winter days are dull and dreary,
Lawns lay heavy with the dew,
Gardens dead and very weary,
Giving the world a dismal view.

Now the north east wind is blowing,
Bringing with it frost and snow,
Hands and faces both get frozen,
Nose nipped and all aglow.

Snow makes the world a pretty picture,
Children toboggan down the hills,
Snowballs, snowmen and maybe skating,
With winter games, their minds are filled.

Winter seems a time of sadness,
Days are dark and nights are long,
Just a glimpse of winter sunshine,
Helps the dreary days along.

The countryside lies quietly sleeping,
Waiting for the signs of spring,
Snowdrops will then come out peeping,
Winter will have had its fling.

Jean Broadley, Wallasey, Merseyside

DRIVER'S LAMENT

Sitting listening to the radio,
Because I've nowhere else to go,
Congestion charges, they're havin' a laugh,
What we need is a place to park,
The only space is on double yellow lines,
Where the yellow peril is issuing fines,
I only stopped to pick up the kids,
It bloody well cost me sixty quid,
Well I'm getting us all bikes,
And I can relax,
Willingly depriving the government,
Of that lovely tax.

Dave Harley, Liverpool, Merseyside

VALUES OF LIFE

My soul is crying,
Whilst my body is dying,
For 'tis too short a life span on Earth.
True love is divine,
War and hate is a crime,
This, only my dream, what it's worth.
To banish all greed, give to those who need,
My eyes long for the seeing of the sight.
To correct such wrongs,
My heart belongs,
With a voice, like a small spark in the night.
Where prejudice is nought,
Only friendship sought.
A prosperous future for man would be seen.
What is that I hear?
Could it be a cheer?
For I think one person knows what I mean

Ken Horton, Wallasey, Merseyside

TAKEN FOR A RIDE

Down on the ferry at the Mersey bay, people get on board
her every day.
A trip across the Mersey to Birkenhead each day, is taken
by people to a regular job,
Or later in the day by the shoppers,
Yes, the ones with a few bob.
Once spring and summer set in, more people
Enjoy a regular ride up and down the Mersey
Admiring the buildings and watching the tide.
Breathing in the air and relaxing on board,
Taking more photos and possibly friends.
To some people it's like getting on a bus or a train,
You know you have to wait but you just get on board,
You haven't got the worries of what can go wrong with your
motor cars.
You can sit back and enjoy your stay,
You know if you enjoy it you'll do the same again another
day.

Patricia McDonough, Sefton, Merseyside

*Dedicated to my father, John McDonough, who was born in
Liverpool. I remember him taking us on the ferry when we
were children.*

Born in Liverpool, **Patricia McDonough** has interests
including writing, drawing and crochet. "I began writing
after an operation and I would describe my style as truth
with feelings," she pointed out. Aged 49, Patricia is disabled
and has an ambition to have her children's stories and
poems published. "I would love to meet a well-known poet
who could help me get my work into print. My worst nightmare is never having my work published," she added.

IF ONLY

If only I could touch you
And feel your gentleness,
As you wiped away my tears
And sorted my distress.

If only I could hear your voice,
Your love for me so strong.
That voice that guided, strengthened me
That never judged me wrong.

If only I could smell you
Your scent of summer flowers.
How you drew me close and held me
For hours and hours and hours.

If only I could taste again
The effort of your fayre,
That daily gave me sustenance
Prepared with loving care.

If only I could see you
Your smile that lit my life,
That banished all my demons
Dear mum, sleep peacefully tonight.

Kathleen Furlong, St Helens, Merseyside

THE LOYAL BREEZE

Came the soothing daily breeze
To cool the sweating land
Travelling on the predatory tide
As it creeps towards the shore

The breeze agrees an amicable arrangement
To undermine the solar heat
Administering its sabbatical medicine
Upon the children of the sun

Sea-gulls bless its kind intervention
As they welcome the sea
As they haggle for permission
To fly the consenting breeze

The breeze revels in adulation
Seduced by the sudden fame
Hearing the complimentary whispers
Born in the private prayers

All day the breeze does operate
In league with the ancient sea
And those who tamed the elements
Are indebted to the loyal breeze

David Bridgewater, Wallasey, Merseyside

NIGHT

Eight o'clock the day is gone,
Stars come out a million to one.
Close the curtains, say goodbye,
Listen to the clock ticking by.
Put your head down to rest,
Knowing that you made the day your best.
Curl up to the one you know,
Off into sleep let your dreams grow.
Images of all good and bad,
You awake to know you are not mad.
The partner of life is still there,
As you lay awake and watch her stare.

Michael Kenneth Barnes, Southport, Merseyside

I WANT TO TELL YOU

I want to tell you something

I want to tell you that your voice is like
the first glug of wine
And like the letters coming through the door.

I want to tell you that up close you draw me in
You are a petal in my side
And I am clay to your touch

I want to tell you that if we were rain drops running down
a window pane
I would let you win

I would find your centre

I would stop being me

Anna Torpey, Wallasey, Merseyside

FRIEND

It is nice to have a friend like you
Who knows just what to say and do
A loving nature so gentle and kind
A friend like you is so hard to find
When our world is dark and we give up the fight
You are the one to switch on the light
To you a problem is but a speck in the mind
Together a solution we will find
Once again the sky is blue
Because we have a friend like you
Who knows just what to say and do

Joan Flynn, Kensington, Merseyside

EMILY

This is a poem for Emily Bronte,
Whose words I have read a thousand times
And have walked with
On your frustrated journey around the table,
Round and round, your foot catching upon the same leg
Every time.
Dreams of roaming free
Across the moors
Wanting to find passion
But never finding
Your Heathcliff,
For I have seen your inspiration,
Felt your repression,
And I have dreamed your torturous death, so young,
So go now and be at one with the nature
You always yearned for
And find your inner peace
My love

Louise Forshaw, Newton-le-Willows, Merseyside

162

PRE-OCCUPIED

He numbly waded past his pear-shaped mantle-mirror,
Failing to recognise his own small distant reflection.
Feelings of loneliness, loss, isolation and abandonment,
Nibbling pounds, hoping for a minute ounce of affection.
Floundering drudgingly through a sad pine-wooded forest,
Yet couldn't recall seeing any of the twisted trees.
Caught out without a coat in a gale-force wind,
And never even felt a breath of the breeze.
Carved out letters with his feet on a beach by an ocean,
Couldn't call to mind what message he'd left in the sand.
Glaring directly into the cruel heart of a relentless
summer's sun,
Gently rubbing away salty tears slowly with his hand.
Wondering where the unity went, they both shared that
was magical,
Or that loving bond they too held secure and sacred.
Now he lays tormented on half of their bed, confused and
fully clothed,
Feeling vacant, sad, betrayed and very naked.

Tommy McBride, Liverpool, Merseyside

*Dedicated to my son, Lee Thomas McBride, for turning his
life around and giving me a beautiful granddaughter,
Cameron Frances McBride.*

Born in Liverpool, **Tommy McBride** has interests including
writing, painting and countryside drives in Wales. "I started
writing when I was a full-time carer for my parents, and in
1999 took creative writing courses at Liverpool University,"
he explained. "I am influenced by Victorian poets and great
men like Bob Dylan, and the people I would most like to
meet are my parents to show them how successful my
poetry has been." Aged 56, Tommy is a retired decorator
with children Lee, Paul, Lisa and Danielle.

DECISIONS

Shades of grey
Outside the pit,
Where I lie
Alone.

I should venture out
Face my fears,
The effects of my mistakes.

But this is easier
Simpler
Shades of black.

Outside is
Dangerous, snarling, angry.
Inside is
Alone with my thoughts
Waiting.

Inside and out bleed together
Should I stand my ground?
Try to run?
Let the end come?

Decisions.

Matthew James Arnold, Formby, Merseyside

SLEEPING OR AWAKE

We walked hand in hand
In the wide open spaces
Which was ours.
In our hills, through our
Streams, and sat by our waters.
So transformed, like children.

Peace in steady paces, in quick
Breath
Happiness out of untameable
Elements.
Calmness in an uphill struggle.
To lose our way was bliss.
To be alive.

We walked to the highest point
Above the clouds.
Where air is clear, and perspective
Fresh.
Freedom enough to make you
Dizzy.
Silence to make you tremble.
Solitude wrapped in love and beauty.

Re-assurance that we can return
Sleeping or awake.

Jennifer Donald, Southport, Merseyside

THE CLIMB

Breath is air as water's sea, a shadow rises beat-by-beat.
Timely journeys on the land dwell conscious spirit hand-in-hand.
I climbed myself up to the sun, a peak of each millennium.
And there the thought which haunts me so, from blood and bone I've come to know,
Upon time there are wonders, but only sadness fills the void of their silence.

Gareth Rogers, Liverpool, Merseyside

Dedicated to my sister Lisa, who I hope finds all the happiness she so very much deserves.

UNIVERSE

Far out in the inky blue heaven
A star twinkles benignly
Hiding infinite power
Masking brilliance from the unquesting mind
Shining like Cubic Zircona

Looking down on a host of golden sons whose attention is focused earthward
Like a congregation with all consuming enthusiasm
Encapsulating life, death, success, failure, love, hate

Memories, shining through eyes of an excited flock, ebb and flow
Soundbites of a billion chanted anthems reverberate
Transmitted down through the generations
Earnest is the belief that the world is captured, conquered
Contained forever, as a priceless jewel

A trillion stars inhabit the Universe and bear witness

June Rose-Hobson, Wallasey, Merseyside

GHOST?

You are the shadow on the stair
The voice I hear when no-one is there.
The whisper in the silent room
The shaft of light, pale in the gloom.
The figure that I thought I saw
But were you there?
I can't be sure.
From the corner of my eye
I see you move, I hear you sigh.
A glint like raindrop in the sun
And then I blink and you are gone.

Frankie Shepherd, Southport, Merseyside

JEKYLL AND HYDE

A jealousy rears its ugly head
Your body's raging, your eyes blood red
Your words exhaling, poison to the air
Which smothers my heart with pain and despair

Your bruised pride is making a stand
My heart is weakened by your anger's demand
Your evil words burn deep in my skin
I can see in you eyes the original sin

Like an eclipse, your face is disguised
From the darkness, tears of remorse you cried
Like a broken child, you fall into my arms
One kiss top my lips and I forget the harm

One glimpse of my weakness
His tears had lied
Goodbye Jekyll
Hello Hyde

Kayleigh Hogg, Liverpool, Merseyside

MEMORIES

Memories of holidays
Skies of blue
People I met
People I knew

Lythe tanned bodies
Ocean washed hair
Smooth skin cosseted
With Ambre Solaire

Skimpy bikinis
Gold ankle chains
Falling in love
Again and again

Flirting and dancing
Into the night
Who really cares
If its wrong or its right

Travelling home
To the cold English mist
But I can remember
When I was truly sun kissed.

Carol Haigh, New Brighton, Merseyside

Dedicated to Gaynor, Susan and Steven with love.

LIFE

Day by day, night by night,
Tick, tock, tick, tock, runs down your life.
Every day should be
Lived and cherished before the flame of life is finally
Extinguished.
No one's life has a guarantee
So smile and laugh and you'll live happily.
When we're gone, we're gone forever.
So make the most of your life because it's now or never.
So when you wake up for another day.
Try to make it a happy one in your own special way.

Anthony Morrin, Netherton, Merseyside

CORRIDORS OF TIME GONE BY

Yellowing
Faded pictures of yesteryear
Evoke a lone nostalgic tear
In these corridors of time gone by

Tiny faces
Forever frozen by the sweeping lens
Teachers, prefects, transient friends
An amalgam of coincidence
In these corridors of time gone by

Yet strangely
What we are now, to a man
Owes something to the fleeting span
Shared with all in this motley clan
Who stare, unseeing from the wall
Between the cloakroom and the hall
In these corridors of time gone by.

M Sargent, Wallasey, Merseyside

FLOWER POWER

I was a sixties flower child or so I like to think.
In hot pants of purple velvet or a pyschadelic pink.
And skinny rib tops low and tight that really were obscene
I strutted into Liverpool as though I were the Queen.

I zipped round in my mini wearing skirts more like a belt
White leather high heel boots, how wonderful they felt.
I wore a lot of cheesecloth and tight pants with a flair
My make-up more like war paint and I straightened my
hair.

My Afghan coat smelt rather strange, it didn't bother me
For life was full of fun with no responsibility.
But now I'm in my fifties and my body's gone to pot
My firm young breasts headed south,
My pants are not right hot.

My hair is white, my legs are veined, skirt is past my knees
My face is filled with laughter lines, from distant memories.
I shop now with my daughters,
They try clothes from off the shelf
Smile, then shiver at their laughter, it's like looking
At myself.

Angela Overend, Heswall, Merseyside

*Dedicated to my children, Chris, Charlie and Louise, for their
inspiration, sense of humour, and love, always.*

FLAT-PACK LAMENT

I've got the flat-pack
And cleared the decks,
I've made two dozen double checks
Uprights two, sides one and two,
And a tube of glue.
An hour later it's all connected,
I feel my work should be respected.
But I look on the floor, and there,
Lies a piece that is obviously spare.
Why?

Barbara Langton, Birkenhead, Merseyside

WRONGED

Dry your eyes my little man,
It's not your fault,
You're not to blame.
One day, you'll know and understand
Life hurts sometimes, real bad.

Those we love can hurt us,
Why? We never really know.
You're safe with me,
I'm always here, to protect and comfort you.

I cannot make your father be the daddy you deserve.
He's wronged you, he knows it.
His silent suffering will eat him alive.
Now let it be.
You need to grow, to learn, to love, to live.
Peace be with you in everything
My brave, beautiful son.

Rose Henry, St Helens, Merseyside

UNTITLED

How do I tell you how I feel?
How do I look into your eyes?
How do I even know this is real?
How do I sleep under these darkened skies?

How can I live without you with me?
How can I exist without your touch?
How can I smile without you near me?
How can I think about you so much?

Sarah Leahey, Liverpool, Merseyside

FEAR

Just for a moment I was in my favourite place
The cool bitter breeze for me to taste
Bright rays of sunlight reflecting on my face
With an earthy smell, trees positioned with grace
The first sunlight allowing me to reminisce past fun
Of summers before but it's no longer the same sun
As the best summers are gone now, I'm growing older
Hold them as memories, now the future looks colder
But as my walk continued, it was strange to occur
My sight and my hearing were unfortunate to blur
Harsh sounds of machines for which I did not care
Buildings on either side of the ground did wear
"Danger," "Death," "Keep out", to my right
My left, "11000 volts" poisoned my sight
Built up around me, I'd walked into the shade
Summers of laughter gone, reasons to be afraid
Thinking about growing up causing a tear
As fibre products causes nature it's own biggest fear

Jessica McClurg, St Helens, Merseyside

LOOKING BACK

I sit on the beach sifting the sand
Running it through my fingers
I think of a distant far off land
And a memory that lingers
I remember the field with a white tent
Where we pitched our marquee
Played from dawn till the sunset went
We were often late for tea

A bike was the transport my dad had
He pulled a wooden trailer
He'd take us to church, pedal like mad
His voice was his loud hailer
Then came the day we went on the train
Parents waving goodbye
We didn't know if we would see them again
Some of us started to cry

I remember the day they said dad had gone
To a better place by far
Look in the sky, you'll see the one
A bright new shining star
Our marquee was given away
To a scout troop who needed it then
My brothers and I would remember that day
Never camp near the beach again

Margaret Lyon, Liverpool, Merseyside

GORGEOUS

Before him, he beheld the vista in all its glory.
No words for this energy, feelings, call it what you will,
that soared, swooped and rested within, soft and still.
The sun rising to its zenith, he was in awe.
Yet there was an other, he felt, not saw.
A father's love freely given; firm his father's hand.
No sound, but simple silence each could understand,
that nature and love and ordinariness all are one.
Then Dad broke the moment, "It's gorgeous, isn't it son?"

Julie Borkwood, Southport, Merseyside

THE KNOWING TREE

The knowing tree,
What do you see?
Something wise and noble as thee.

Through timeless days
You stand and observe.
Passing decades,
And nature's curves.

The seasons change your appearance to us,
Dressing you up and then leaving you bare.
Yet still you will stand there, strong and tall,
Keeping a record of it all,
Until it is your time to fall.

L M Boyd, Knowsley, Merseyside

*Dedicated to my lovely family, husband Ray, children
Christian and Jessica, with fondest memories of my dear
dad, Harry White.*

THE PUB NOWADAYS

If you go to the pub nowadays
You will see that they have changed.
In some parts they sell cakes and tarts
They don't even let you play darts.
If you go to the pub nowadays.

They don't let you tell dirty jokes,
They laugh at you if you buy some smokes.
They say you must not stand by the bar,
That you don't drink and drive the car.
They look like cafes
Whatever happened to the laughs.
If you go to the pub nowadays.

They are open all day
Where do they get the money to pay.
Excuse me can you pass the ash tray
Sorry pal you cannot smoke in here.
For goodness sake its just not fair,
They say it gets on your clothes and in your hair.

I remember when it closed at three
You and your mates go home for your tea.
Then you got your head down
So you were ready to go down town,
And let your hair down.
But not if you go to the pub nowadays.

Joey Langton, Liverpool, Merseyside

UNTITLED

Cheer up it may not happen
And even if it should
You wouldn't find it half as hard
As now you think you would.
For troubles are but bubbles
And they may seem rather rum.
But you'll find life's biggest troubles
Are the ones that never come.

Mary Angela Miller, Formby, Merseyside

RESTLESS NIGHT

Lying here in my bed
Lots of things going through my head
For hours now I have tried to sleep
My eyes are sore now and starting to weep
I glance across at my sleeping wife
She's probably just dreaming about everyday life
I get out of bed looking for things to do
I look at the clock, it's just after two
I go downstairs to make a drink
The pain in my eyes are making them blink
I sit at the table to read a book
It's a murder mystery about a cook
I put on the kettle to make some tea
I look at my watch, it's nearly three
I'm feeling tired and really stressed
Soon be time for me to get dressed
I look out the window, it's starting to get light
Just another restless night

Robert Evans, Liverpool, Merseyside

GOT ANY GUM CHUM?

They march, those cheerful black platoons of soldiers,
lick spit smart.
Faces split with huge wide grins,
singing in joyful counterpart.
Welcomed and feted, in this cold grey land
made austere by adversity.
Come to lend a hand,
to fight, and conquer the enemy.
The children stand, awed by the numbers,
stand in their worn tired clothes.
And soldiers, shocked by the devastation,
call to them, "You want candy?"
Looking around at burnt out buildings,
in consternation.
How tired these children look, how thin,
but with an unconquerable spirit still.
Slowly, slowly, the line snakes through to the Bootle
station,
disappearing, and the roads and streets go silent.
How many of these willing fighters,
soldiers, saviours all heaven sent,
will live, to sing and smile, and after sacrifice,
go home from beaches,
named for their own Home Lands, their Paradise.

Lynda Day Bidston, Bootle, Merseyside

*Dedicated to Mayla Williams Day, my mother, who lived
through the conflict*

THE WALK

As I walked along the road
Getting nearer to my abode.
I saw a woman crying tears
She told me her troubles and all of her fears.
She picked up her basket and gave me some bread
She said "Don't be famished or you will be dead."
So I got out my soup that I had bought that day
And we ate all the food as we went on our way.

Albert E J Carpenter, Birkenhead, Merseyside

FIRE

I start off as a merry flame
To keep you warm and cosy,
But as I roar through your house, I get the blame,
Your only hope is neighbours being nosy.
My inner body holds layers of which you'll never find,
So keep on adding wood in your leisure,
And let me catch it in my bind.
I am a force you cannot measure.
I ruin the city, raise it to the ground,
I lick the sides of castle walls,
Then shoot round and round
And watch amused as it falls.
I am something everyone fears
And of all the things, I am no liar,
I reduce people to tears,
I am fire.

Rachael Ross, Birkenhead, Merseyside

Dedicated to my mum and dad. Thank you for everything.

MOONSHINE BABE

We kissed then climbed into the car
Myself knowing it would take her afar.
We drove all morning and arrived at ten
To the echoing sound of London's Big Ben.

The plane's departure was not till eleven
As me and her dad stared at heaven.
"Don't go," I remember saying into your ears.
As I felt something trickle, one of my tears.

We walked for a while clung to each other
Then you talked about a ham shank,
And I said don't bother.
To fulfil an ambition you had to be strong
Deep down I felt it had to be wrong.

We entered the airport in a terrible state.
With you crying, and me asking you to wait.
Up the long corridors, down the moving stairs.
As your dad tried to comfort me saying "Don't despair."

The end was near as we stopped at the gate.
We kissed for ages, and I told you I would wait.
You held my hands then slipped away
I glared at the runway and sobbed in dismay.
I cherish the day when you return
To be my wife and not Miss Burns.

Matthew Paul De-Gier, Liverpool, Merseyside

MY

Creeping carriage caresses corners,
Clandestine and crafty,
Sleekly slipping, soft and silent,
Silhouetted shadow.
Teasing terror, tensely treading,
Tentatively taunting?

Meow

Rebecca Jackson, Wallasey, Merseyside

A TYPICAL TEEN?

Dis' moi crew,
Hangin' in me hood,
Copper's just come,
Kicked us up the bum,
Ain't done jack,
Man we ain't like tha'.

It ain't really fair,
We don't do pot,
Still they don't care.

It's the way I parle,
Init? The gear I wear,
But man, I don't swear.

Ya say ya scared,
Of me an' ma crew,
But hey there dude,
What I done to you?

Gill Hulse, Southport, Merseyside

UNTITLED

Do you remember Kirkby when
Everyone worked and men were men
Towerhill meant maisonettes
The rent strike and all those debts

The Kirkby show was a great day out
Fortunetellers and a boxing bout
Tombola, the waltzers, prizes galore
Then the Morris dancers hit the floor

Remember the schools, Rushey-Hey and St Mick's
Then you got to St Kevs and weren't you big licks
There not there now they've been raised to the ground
But Brookfield and Ruffwood are as sound as a pound

The cut old Ingoe lane in two
Coz the M57 was coming through
They took away the stockcar track
They say its progress we want them back

I know its forward that I must look
Coz in this community a vow I took
To love my neighbour and we'd stay strong
Coz with Kirkby people you can't go wrong

Brenda Clarke, Kirkby, Merseyside

*Dedicated to my Mum, Violet Rowan, who worked in
Westvale school for many years as a much-loved dinner
lady.*

ME AND MY ASBO

My mum is 28
Nana's old at 41
For my 16th birthday
I get my first ASBO

All the girls
Have got one
And the lads do too
Maybe you have seen us
We are trouble and taboo

We drink, we smoke
We sleep about
And we take drugs too

On street corners
We do sit
Oh and we love a fight
Doesn't matter, who it's with
Depends on the night

My "step dad" says I'm wicked
And "really" he should know
Cause fifteen step kids, he has
Got each with their own ASBO

Suzanne Flynn, Huyton, Merseyside

Dedicated to my mum. RIP, and a massive thank you to Keith.

SUMMER DAYS

Whisper to the silence of a dream.
For so it would seem and many years since passed.
Of days long gone, they were never meant to last.
I close my eyes, trying to capture the past.
Childhood, happy memories, endless laughter on the beach.
Stretch out my arms and reach for the deep blue sea to caress my soul.
My heart never letting go, just daydreaming, I know.
Once again the wind brushing through my hair.
Creating a vision that can almost take me there.
Sunsets woven, golden grains running through my finger tips.
Salty breeze in the air, gently places a single kiss upon my lips.
Run! Long locks flowing, suntanned skin, healthy and glowing.
Watching the tide, slowly, in and out, waves rolling.
Child lost in time and from another land.
Long summer days, baking hot sand.
With a bucket and spade, you grew older, slowly fading away.
I remember, I can still see you play.

Jo Goddard, Warrington, Cheshire

DREAMS

Fly in your dreams and find me
I will be waiting for you
On the beach of angels
Hurry to my side, my love

Ray Owens, Runcorn, Cheshire

THE CARPENTER

A day came when I held my father's jackplane,
the salt grout of his sweat on heavy beech.
I worked a face and edge on a cedar balk
that breathed the resin of dark woods
and showed the tracery of grain
made from the sun and wind, the night rain and the cold
rain,
the dendrochronology of being.

I'm given, since, to workshop twilight, the small window
looking upon trees, the sun and wind, the night rain and
the cold rain,
where timbers through the dust give scent according to
their kind
and carry in their flesh dead chronicles of times
and contour lines of dreams nobody had.
Out of these happenings I'll make you tables, cribs and
toys
not knowing how my right angle of reason
comes by the window to a thing
made of the sun and wind, the night rain and the cold rain.

John Dixon, Neston, Cheshire

CHOUGHED

Red, vermillion, scarlet beak and claw
Black, shining, iridescent feathers more
Soaring, gliding, stalling high
Right up there in the sky

Turning, curling, winding, circling round
Enjoying flying well above the ground
I am free from all the earth up here
A black spirit water reflect in mere

Julian Warwick, Northwich, Cheshire

JUKEBOX

Jukebox
You must have played
So many mighty records in your time
For the liners and the diners
In this lonely greasy grime
Sucking on their ciggies
As you sing their favourite song
You survived the jump and jive
And you're still going strong
You must have seen
So many generations come and go
Even there to celebrate
The birth of rock 'n' roll
Standing in the corner
Of this smoky luncheonette
Even when we're dead and gone
You'll still be there I bet
Jukebox
The great almighty jukebox

Rod Trott, Nantwich, Cheshire

RAIN

If rain could tell our stories,
Then mine would surely be,
Sadness, anger and confusion,
Falling down on me.

If rain could be our best friend,
Then mine would surely be,
A happy, fun and cool person,
Just to make up for me.

But rain can't do the above,
So I'll leave you here to ponder
What the hidden meaning of my poem might be.

Zita Abila, Sale, Cheshire

LIKE CLOUDS

Hitch a ride on a cloud so wide
Let it take you to another side
And leave this place that has no place
To keep you chained in life denied
Go float away and don't look down
Dream your fate in an open space
And don't you listen to doubts that lied
Just lay your head on a soothing grey
Let it lift you to a better day
And claim your right that has no right
To heap shadows upon your glowing ray
Fall gently in it's wool-like folds
And dreaming drift your troubles gone
Like clouds they come and blow away

Mark Hogan, Runcorn, Cheshire

GOSSAMER

The stone grey turrets of the tower
Arise amid the trees
The mists of an October morn
Like wisps around the leaves
Of red and gold the copper bronze
Of autumn fantasies

And through the mists of tide and time
A greater glory breathes
Of heavenly love abiding peace
And restful sanctuaries
And quiet blessings drift my way
From the church tower in the trees

Beryl Leece, Wallasey, Cheshire

A SENSE OF LOSS

An empty bus stands idling at its stop
The dying high street of a textile town
Faint yellow lines creep past a factory shop
Mist settles on the hills and rain comes down
On passengers who just arrived too late
From silent streets where orange twilight falls
The driver pulls away and will not wait
Youths shelter by graffiti-covered walls

Two chairs, a wooden table and a jug
Of milk, a sugar bowl, a china pot
Some crumbs of cake, a solitary mug
Its handle chipped, its contents barely hot
And, leaning on that single cup of tea
A card that reads "With deepest sympathy"

David Favager, Bebington, Cheshire

AN UNDERSTANDING

You are the robin, the sun, the sky,
The gentle breeze where sparrows fly.
The rolling waves and rippling tides,
A small, warm house where love abides.
Your love is like the flowers of spring,
Bringing light to everything.
You are the sunny daffodil, but in the end,
Strong winds come to buffet and bend.
But you hold on, there's always hope,
I wish I could stop the wind, help you cope.
But the wind goes on and on down life's track,
Until it wins and you can't bounce back.

Christine Rowley, Winterley, Cheshire

SCATTER MY ASHES

Scatter my ashes to the fair winds that blow
Whether in sunshine or whether in snow
Then I beg you
Don't stand and weep
I will not be there
I'll never sleep
I'll be in your happy laughter
Ringing out of all your doors
I'll be in the purple heather
As you tramp amongst the moors
I'll be in the sparkling crystal sea
As you swim and bathe so young and free
So be happy for the life I've led
Rejoice, I'm with the Lord
And as you kneel by your bed
All I ask of thee is...
That with love you'll remember me

Janet Jones, Poynton, Cheshire

AMBER

Suspended in an amber gold,
The insect, like a scarab, lies,
Seduced from time; forever more,
Suspended in an amber gold,
That glitters like a distant shore.
Although outside each moment flies,
Suspended in an amber gold,
The insect, like a scarab, lies.

Reginald Waywell, Warrington, Cheshire

SAINT AMONGST SINNERS

When the rivers run red
And the sky becomes fire
And the weapons of war
Are now your messiah
When the poets are dead
All the heroes are lost
Every word is deceit
And every truth has its cost
Will you run in fear
Or fight in vain
Shed a tear for the dead ones
Or try to sustain
A world that is breaking
Where hope never came
As the slow years pass
They won't remember your name

Sophie Kavanagh, Stockport, Cheshire

LARGER THAN LIFE

When I look in a mirror
What do I see?
An overweight woman
Looks back at me

When in front of the camera
At a family do
I hide at the back
Well out of view

What man would want
A woman so flabby?
My self-esteem's low
I feel so unhappy

My diet is poor
Coke, burgers and chips
The measuring tape
Won't fit around my hips

I desire a man
Who is fit and athletic
But who would want me?
I'm utterly pathetic

Diane Burrows, Failsworth, Greater Manchester

MY DISABILITY WONT BEAT ME

It controls my life,
Limits what I can do,
But it will never beat me,
That's one thing it cannot do.

I want to go to college,
To learn and to act,
You've never stopped me before,
You've never had an impact.

It will be used to stop me,
It will be a barrier in my way,
But I've beaten it before,
And continue to do so each day.

But I'm saying 'Thankyou'
For my disability has given me power,
Never to give up easily.
Yes, I'll have my hour.

I'm going to be an actress,
It'll be a challenge to face,
But I've beaten Cerebral Palsy,
And I'll win this at my pace.

Vicki Wroe, Prestwich, Greater Manchester

THE STEAM TRAIN

The roar of the fire, the shovelling of coal
The smell of grease in times of old.
The gushing of steam the trains away
A new destination day by day.
The turning of the wheels as she goes by
I wish they were the trains I could drive.

Gloria Hamlett, Swinton, Greater Manchester

WHO'S THAT GIRL?

I stare in the mirror,
Looking at what my expression is saying,
My eyes so blank,
'Cause a large wall blocks any emotion.
A face so down, but it smiles to make people happy,
Yet only I know,
That the smile is not for happiness but sadness,
Trying to look the part for other people's attention,
Then all that they see is the person on the outside,
And not the person on the inside which really matters.
The mirror shows a lot and tells a lot,
My expression tells me unhappy things,
It shows my pain, shows my fears,
The mirror tells the cold truth
That you hate to hear,
Every once in a while,
Look into the mirror,
Because your expression does not lie.

Victoria Webb, Oldham, Greater Manchester

PRESENT COMPANY REJECTED

When we were young, life was easier,
No broken hearts, bones or seizures.
Take it all away from me
So I can have my liberty
I've been blinded too many times
By beautiful guys
With pleasures in mind,
Only to be dashed and sometimes bashed.
It's a mess but it's mine,
No-one to blame but me,
Same old same all the time,
No-one plays straight down the line.
On my terms and in my time,
Life I know can be real fine.
Strawberry days and vodka nights,
Are you brave enough to turn out the lights?
Remember, no-one knows how the future goes,
But the man who is true in spirit grows.

Darren Anthony Stoker, Manchester

MY BUSY LIFE

STOP
For a moment, time to reflect,
Phone won't stop ringing, jobs not done yet.
Work on my mind, so much to do,
Will my "to do" list ever be through?
Mum has been calling, can't seem to find,
Time to catch up she's on my mind.
A treadmill of get ups, bells and deadlines,
Shopping and juggling, cramming up my time.
Husband at home, rarely time to talk,
Hair in a mess, hands covered with chalk.
Home always second, job always first,
Is it really so important, lining my purse?

Nicky Lewis, Sale, Greater Manchester

SPRING GARDEN

A promise of summer, the bright spring sun
Rainbows the drops from the showers which splash
Across the garden in fierce bursts to lash
The flowers and shrubs before the children run
For shelter to the drooping willow tent beside the pond
Then soon again, the sunbright world returns
And fresh washed bluebells swing allied
With swaying cowslips in the grass, while the ferns
Within the rockery uncurl their fresh green tendrils
The lilac bush beside the fence, a perfumed ledge
Where bluetits launch their flight and hone their skills
To catch the caterpillars for their mate in hole or hedge
The shifting trees, the zephyr breeze brings sunlit hours
Along the branches, down the path, the squirrels chase
Each other up and down until the showers
Return again to water all the plants which grow apace

Norma Edwards, Stockport, Greater Manchester

VICIOUS LIES OF PURPLE

Purple is my head, my anger ripe,
Harvesting the vicious lies I was told.
Purple are my hands, tense and sore,
Aching to rip the lips which spout
Vicious lies that were told.

Purple is my heart, burning,
With rage pumps so loud, I am deafened,
My heart is mangled by the
Vicious lies that were told.

Purple are my toes, curl up and tremble,
So sore in my shoes, damn those
Vicious lies I was told.

And purple are my eyes which cry,
So much I am blind with
The vicious lies I was told.

Anna Sabti, Didsbury, Greater Manchester

A LOVE SO DIVINE

From me to you
From you to me
A rotation of love
Surrounding our lives
Protecting our hearts
Bonding two hearts together into one
Creating pleasure and happiness
For this beautiful couple
Who's love is so divine

Andrew Rawlings, Oldham, Greater Manchester

UNTITLED

The mills are filled with smoke,
So much I could choke.
The pieces are working on their strings,
They aren't allowed to speak,
So they dare not sing.
The factory owner whips the children all about,
All you feel like doing
Is going to the owner to shout.
"Outside there are people dying,
And think of all that trying,
The rich Victorians think the poor are scum,
I think they should pity their mums"
When you see the children dying,
All you do is start crying.
I'm glad I'm not in the Victorian times
Because of all the badness they had,
It makes you feel very sad.

Paige Dady, Salford, Greater Manchester

REFLECTIONS

Is he the man that I once knew,
When I was young, with clearer view,
His mark upon the world to make,
But time, a thief, his youth would take.

With vigour, hope, and new found dreams
This man could conquer all, it seems,
But as with every passing day,
The debt of time, the price, he'd pay.

Did he achieve his plans and dreams,
A few, I think, or so it seems,
And still within his aging mind,
Are goals to gain, if life is kind.

Look hard again and recognise,
This mans reflections, old but wise,
The man you see that once you knew,
Is times reflection friend, of you.

L Chisnall, Salford, Greater Manchester

ETERNAL MUSIC

Makes you feel a sense of worth,
Artificial truth is heard.
Your body feels it, moves in time,
Your mind is warped,
Your soul divine,
A minute in eternity,
Is worth a thousand seconds free,
You'd kill for just a moment more,
But then you knowingly deplore.
An instant's worth unending notes,
For rare is sweeter as we know,
So timeless in a false made truth,
Eternal music will bear fruit.

Hayley Jones, Stockport, Greater Manchester

MOTHER AND SON

On the last day of May,
I saw you from the high windows,
A red and blue speck screened by tall poplar trees.
Her bright gold buttons glistened in the sunlight like
dubloons.
While sunglasses provided soft shade and privacy.
You sat contented, often no need for conversation,
For the birdsong and distant cars were music enough.
Above, the milky-blue sky remained cloudless,
While all around, clusters of rhododendron bushes
Blossomed in profusion.
And as I watched, I marvelled how you merged with the
landscape,
At peace with nature, in all its beauty and tranquillity.
In perfect symmetry forever.

Felicia Rochelle Isaacs, Whitefield, Greater Manchester

MY TIME, MY PLAY

My story begins with a birth,
A new character in the age old play,
Already the ending's predicted,
But let the journey have its say.

Scene one plays out an emotion,
A simple drama of improvisation.
Now the cast is selected and the stage set,
It's time for the director's creation.

My play twists and turns,
Scattering plot lines and people.
The fragments of love, fear and laughter,
Blend with the cries for a sequel.

I rewind on old moments,
Fast forward to a blank screen,
But regrets and understanding,
Muddled with hope, confuse the dream.

Louise Butler, Oldham, Greater Manchester

MY FUTURE

The future can be bright
And all things seem right
Until there's a slight
Twist to the plot
Should I do this or not?
A wrongly taken decision
Could easily cause
Future strife for me
And all around me
With their actions and reactions
To my change of mind
This marriage is done and dusted
It must be left behind
For all out sakes except his

Andrea King, Rochdale, Greater Manchester

MOVING HOUSE

Moving brings a sadness of things that will be gone.
You are giving up your home, you are moving on.
I first remember moving when I was only nine
We moved from town to country, left behind the grime.
I missed my friends and relatives, lamented every day
For familiar voices and faces passing on their way.
Little snippets of music, the odd dogs bark.

The rattle of a steam train, boys shouting in the park.
To a quieter setting with nothing going on,
The people were strangers to me and I was all alone.
I have moved many times since and it becomes true,
That it is never as hard as the first time.
Just simply new.

Barbara Jardine, Oldham, Greater Manchester

A COMPANION I NEED FOR A LIFETIME

That loving gaze I need from you
My heart seeks to live in your heart
Keep smiling at me just like this
Keep smiling at me
I need support for a lifetime
My heart seeks to live in your heart

You are my sweetheart, you are my God
You are different, you are apart
What gift must I give you? Where every lover gives his
heart?
My life, I will lay down for you should you ever need it
My heart seeks to live in your heart

On my own I shall go to seed
Without your shelter I will die
This is not merely a journey through millions of lifetimes
Through this journey I need a companion
My heart seeks to live in your heart

Naheed Nadeem, Rochdale, Greater Manchester

FAIRY FOLK

I believe in fairies, yes I really do.
Some kind of a fairy lives in you.
Gentle little people, with hearts of gold.
Graceful and kind, with a peaceful mind.

Cuddle and happy with imagination and
Hair, colourful locks of sweet smelling hair.
Soft petals glide past and gently touch a face,
Glittery fairy dust disappears without a trace.

Sitting on a pure white flower, my mind finds
Stillness for half an hour.
All you fairy folk all around, listening
To the thoughts of others without any sound.

Yvette Parker, Ashton-under-Lyne, Greater Manchester

SIMPLICITY

Plain and simple language,
That is all I ask.
Is it too much to expect,
A plain and simple task?

No call for arduous locutions
That no-one can perceive,
Or long and detailed sentences
That people can't believe.

I like simple vocab,
Easy reading, nothing tedious,
Only flowing streams of words,
Assisted by my thesaurus.

Jean Hopwood, Middleton, Greater Manchester

A NOVEMBER POEM

I hate this month, my neighbour said,
There is no colour, everything is dead.
As she stood by the cornus stems
And rhus typhinus leaves of red.

And the hebe flowers still purply-blue,
The last summer insects buzz
Over flowers of sedum, too.

Pale yellow sun spotlights through grey clouds
The leaves from the birch
Twirling to the ground
To cambrian poppies still around.

I hate this month,
There is no colour anyway.
Standing by the apple tree,
With trunk of green and grey.

There's forty shades of green, they say,
But you're aware of none today.
Are we so different, you and me?
You cannot see what I can I see.

Doris Thomson, Middleton, Greater Manchester

IN CYBERWIND

It appeared
In the bedroom window view

A slender, weed like thing
Barely effacing the summer efflux from buildings.

It pricked there,
The persistent intruder,

The following morning against uncertain bluey tape,
Against the pink blanche of twilight.

Through scopes
It arrayed its dish; the straight bi-polar surprise.

It was there
To suck and send

The blather of a world shrunk
In conspectus and expectation
To that of a slug:

Slow, but fast; feed me.

How the slithery gobbling creatures congregate
To their masts of coolness.

Another threat on the horizon.

Robert Burgess, Manchester, Greater Manchester

APRIL TIME

An April morning, the first light of dawn,
Stealing over the tree tops, an April day is born.
Flooding the city, this unearthly light,
Spears of sunbeams, shimmering bright.
Borders of tulips on colourful parade,
Clusters of daisies, all in white arrayed.
Masses of bluebells, a startling view,
Covering the woodlands, an enchantment in blue.
Carried on the air, a fragrant perfume,
Apple blossom, now in full bloom.
The petals falling down from the trees,
Floating and dancing on the breeze.
Out of clear blue skies, the sudden showers,
Like sparkling crystals, washing the flowers.
Leaving glistening pearl drops on every bush,
As if painted with a magical brush.
As pretty as a picture, April time,
Following natures rhythm and rhyme.
The air, the light, and the early morning dew,
As if all the earth were starting anew.

Miriam Duddridge, New Moston, Greater Manchester

CHASING THE MOON

Childhood wishes and fairytale dreams.
Memories in a scrap book,
That bursts at the seams.
On the swings in the park.
Snuggled up in winter,
When outside is dark.
Building a fort
That is fit for a king.
Up a tree so high
You can hear the birds sing.
So wonderful is childhood
It's over soon.
But remember how fun it was
Chasing the moon.

Sarah Louise Smith, Blackley, Greater Manchester

A THANKLESS TASK

There are invisible men around our streets
Cleaning up rubbish from beneath our feet.
It's a thankless task I think you'll agree
Moving God knows what
They really earn their fee.

Toffee papers and sometimes worse
Keeping our streets free from dirt.
As they go from street to street
I'll bet they work up a real good thirst.

But some-one has to do it,
And it's praise to them all
I'm only glad it's not me.

Pauline Ann Green, Leigh, Greater Manchester

UNTITLED

Some are born with good luck,
For others it's something acquired,
But for one or two unfortunate ones,
In its denial the fates have conspired.

There's someone I knew for example,
Whose luck was just non-existent,
With no sign of a break whatsoever,
His run of bad luck was consistent.

His misfortune ended quite suddenly,
When he stepped in front of a bus,
As a result of that error,
I'm afraid he's no longer with us.

At last he's been blessed with some luck,
He's in heaven, awaiting a place
He's perched on a shelf by the entrance,
While inside they find him a space.

That's not the end of the story,
For when he climbed down from the shelf,
He was picked out for reincarnation,
And sent back to earth as himself.

Richard Dunne, Liverpool, Merseyside

MATRIMONY

Not my problem
Nothing to do with me,
Go and sort it
Just let me be.
Mind your own business
Keep your nose out,
Don't make me angry
Don't make me shout.
Now I'm frustrated
Why can't you see?
You want some support
You'll not get it from me.

Norma Wilson, Southport, Merseyside

DOWN

Defeat,
Despair,
Division all discarded.
Deutschland's youth from east and west
Gather at the wall,
Gather on the wall
To witness its demise.
Brandenburg, gate to nowhere
For more years than they can remember.
Brandenburg, gate to a future
For today's inheritors of yesterday's wrongs.
Together, hand-in-hand atop the wall
They grasp the moment when the concrete crumbles,
Crushed in the jaws of mechanical might.
Together, they erase that scar, scar upon their nation,
Together, stand to watch with bated breath,
Emotion briefly stifling an exultant roar.

Lesley Michell, St Helens, Merseyside

ONE MORNING AT CHURCH

I sat in church the other day,
Perhaps I am too old to sing and pray.
I gazed around and this I'll say,
Most of the heads were going grey.
There were more old folk, than those who were young
Where are those people, whose lives have just begun.
Hardly any young people, that I could see
Lots of crabby ones, very much like me.
In twenty years time will all this fade away?
Too late will it be then for the vicar to pray.
If our religion is to be kept alive,
Now is the time to make it revive.

Albert E Bird, Southport, Merseyside

OUR GARDENS

Incredible colours greet our gaze
Green branches silhouette the sprays
Blossoms hang from bowers and screens
Where white magnolias can be seen

Down each slope, majestic trees
Sway so stately in the breeze
Around each curve a new delight
Red, yellow, peach and blue so bright

Bluebells peep from bush and fern
In tranquil ponds, fish laze and turn
Fresh waterfalls cascading down
To tumbling stones, smooth and round

For all of nature's precious store
Help us God to care much more

Doreen M Evans, Southport, Merseyside

LOST DREAMS

The azure skies that sail
Softly past my mind,
Searching for your face
Which brings the sunshine.
You feel alive inside the mind of a child.
The lines under your eyes
Come out more in the morning light,
The dreams which you had
Cress your hair and fall to the ground.
If you don't encore them to the edge,
They will fade away without a sound.

Anthony Atkinson, Liverpool. Merseyside

ABSENT

Sex and lust are the words that accompany me
Everywhere I go.
My stomach goes a flutter when I scurry around,
Like the leaves off the trees.
They are fleeing away from their libido.
I want to banish you to the hills,
I can't take any more of your reluctant love.

Being in two minds about you, would be blatant enough.
You are the essence of love.
I wish I was deprived permanently
Rather than have to accept this torture.
You offend me every time you leave.
Your departure leaves me awkward.
Your love makes me jump, especially when you run.
Don't run away from me.
It's a relief to see you, but then you just say goodbye.
No number of kisses.

Yvonne St Clair, Liverpool, Merseyside

THE PANIC BUTTON

Around a neck once long, unlined,
And often kissed and stroked,
A simple necklace, black and red,
Nestles in wrinkled folds
No diamonds, gold, no pearls, no kiss,
Around her neck but still
In dreams she fingers auburn curls,
Wakes mindful of forgotten thrill.
Jewellry loathsome to the eye,
A mill stone to remind of death,
The day it's touched, the day to die,
A buzz, a gasp, a final breath.

Paul Yates, Lydiate, Merseyside

HUMAN NATURE

We each have a story,
A tale of our life.
Our hopes and our dreams,
Of troubles and of strife.
A moment remembered,
A tear in your eye,
The thought of deception.
That shame, that lie.
We share in successes,
Our ego we pad.
We wallow in the sad times,
Cry when we're bad.
We each have our own world,
That space, that retreat,
Where we go when we're honest,
And its ourselves we must meet.

Colin McCombe, Moreton, Merseyside

HOME IS WHERE THE HEART IS

Home is where the heart is,
That's where mine waits for me,
Home is what I long for,
That's where I want to be,
I don't want to be here any longer,
Lying in a mass grave,
For that's all the trenches are,
A place of death for the young and brave,
I'm not alone in my hell,
My friends are here with me,
We stand and fight together,
For the homes we can no longer see.

Jennie Bullock, Kensington, Merseyside

SORRY

I found an old photograph,
Of you the other day.
Now I've sat to write this,
I can't think of what to say.
A lot of tears have fallen,
When I thought of you,
So writing these words,
Is all I could think to do.
I know perhaps I'd hurt you,
And things got really bad,
But I always remember,
The happy times we had.
I can only apologise,
Don't know what else to do,
Except to say my daughter,
The next move is up to you.

Marilynne Harrison, Rock Ferry, Merseyside

LOVING THOUGHTS

Whilst merged in hushed quietness,
Deep in thoughts of freedom, nothing less.
My happiness, gently appealing,
Fills my heart with a romantic feeling.

My loving thoughts I send today,
Gladly they will travel your way.
Though we are many miles apart,
They come direct from my heart.

This may take some time to reach you,
My wish please treat these thoughts as true.
I send my devoted love to you.
Trusting you are thinking of me too.

Dearest I know your love for me,
Hand in hand let hearts agree.
The future together is my dream,
To enhance our life to a loving theme.

With my ardent thoughts, I now propose,
Knowing your future is with me too.
With sweet good wishes, I now close,
As always my fondest love to you.

Harry Boyle, Southport, Merseyside

MODERN LIVES

People rush about each day,
There is no time to sit or stay,
People to see, places to go,
They have to rush, they daren't be slow.
They don't have time to sit and stare,
Look at life, breathe in the air,
They never stop to look around,
The birds in flight, life in the ground.
Busy lives we all do lead,
We take too much in our selfish greed,
Take some time to sit and study,
There is no need to rush and hurry.
Before too long it will all be gone,
Then we will realise what we have done.

Pam Lewis, Bootle, Merseyside

SONNET

Minds are more aware than discerning eyes,
Attractions forged by a beautiful face
Can sometimes cease, when beauty fades and dies,
How can you know if love is true or false.
Love, where are you from? Do you oft wonder
Why, when passion is spent the mind is calm,
Yet, how can I speak of this with candour,
When I know not the measure of love's charm.
A faithful love, can one be forgotten?
How can emotion be measured by gain,
The last offering to man begotten
for ultimate joy, and tormenting pain.
Will our world ever be wearied of love?
A precious free gift from heaven above.

Arthur Bradbury, St Helens, Merseyside

SWEETHEART'S DEMISE

Oh pray be still and calm my tiring heart;
Stir not within, leave me to remember,
Joyful memories, past tryst, true confer,
My undying love, yet temporary apart,
Sunshine, life, warmth, once my soul mate I sought,
For life I could not think, reason gentler.
Now gone, I to untold depths do sink for her;
Against thy beauty, were I crude in thought.
Perfection, justice could I not perform.
Oh how memory tempts my feeble mind.
I resist not, in seeps your essence warm;
Love I long for, left me forlorn, unkind.
Tenderly slipped my sweetheart, oh so worn;
Left, a dark shadow, yet still ties that bind.

D Parry, Wallasey, Merseyside

SCIATICA

Sciatica's an awful thing,
If you've had it you'll agree;
It starts beneath the spine
And works its way down to the knee;
The tibia and fibula do not escape the pain,
Which when it reaches boiling point,
]Could send you quite insane.
For ten weeks now I've suffered it,
My weight has dropped away,
To all you "would be dieters"
Sciatica's the way.
So if you're really desperate,
To get a slim waist line,
Don't hesitate to contact me,
And I'll hand over mine.

Jean Shingler, Southport, Merseyside

A THOUGHT BEFORE I SLEEP

How can a day be so short?
Sometimes passing like a thought.
Hours moving fast, lost to the past,
A new day starts like it ought.

As midnight marks the day's end,
I'm left here thinking of a friend.
A love so dear, I want her near,
So in my dreams I'll pretend.

Daniel Cheung, Liverpool, Merseyside

FATHER FIGURE

The figure looks as it's the fathers
Son don't turn to the bottle then fight.
Why do they steal from each other?
This is a rough view of what a broken home is like.

She must take after her mother
Because they both can't meet Mr Right
Will they ever have a true lover?
This is a rough view of what a broken home is like.

Can you mend a broken home,
Or a broken heart?
Have you got the hands?
Do you hold the key?

Sisters locked out by their brother.
And so they seem terrified day and night.
Should they only care for one another?
This is a rough view of what a broken chain is like.

Larissa Weston, Liverpool, Merseyside

MISTAKES

Slowly as time trickled by,
I saw my life flash past.
Another trickle, another flash,
Memories I shed like tears.

The silence screams inside of me,
Drowning in the need for affection.
Raging with insanity,
My dull eyes weep.

Wishing to cling to you for support,
Your hand to rest in mine.
Like a small child I feel wanted,
And unprecious at the same time.

The future so close to the mistakes of the past,
Like a ship setting off with a broken sail.
Overwhelmed with renewed fear I feel,
My heart slowly fading.

Don't go sprinting off to unknown waters,
Stay where your heart's content.
This mistake is often made,
By the likes of me.

Kelly Hellon, Birkenhead, Merseyside

THE BLUEBELL WOOD

The beech tree, noble and serene,
Unfolds its leaves of brightest green,
And there, beyond the old oak tree,
Flowers of loveliest hue I see,
Bluebells, spreading an azure carpet
Beneath the canopy of trees,
Wafting their sweet fragrance on the gentle breeze.
Of springtime's riches can aught compare
With this bluebell wood, so rich and fair?

Marjorie Lomax, St Helens, Merseyside

I WATCH YOU

All night I watch you from across the room
Never daring to bridge our distance.
You hold court with vibrant conversation
Lighting up each face that nears you.
You laugh and drink and smoke,
Blowing out fascination with each puff.
And I adore you,
Even though I don't know your name.

All too soon, your cab arrives and you exit
Followed by your admiring entourage.
But my legs hold me to the spot
Like hardened lead,
And I cannot follow.

I gulp down my drink
And it chokes me.

I will never know your name.

Dawn L Edwards, Liverpool, Merseyside

I'M HERE

I have never lost a loved one
So I don't know how you feel,
They say that it gets easier
And time can make it heal.

I cannot give you reassurance
And say that this is true,
Because that would be empty words
That you would see right through.

You can try to hide your grief
And paint a smile upon your face,
Or show that you are brave
To the rest of the human race.

I can see a bit deeper
And I know you are feeling pain.
So I will try to help you through
Until you can smile again.

So remember I am here
For you to always depend.
To listen to a memory
Or simply be a friend.

Cathy Dwyer, Liverpool, Merseyside

DON'T SMOKE

The pleasure of smoking is hard to explain
But the feeling of cancer's a definite pain.
So before you drag on your next cigarette,
Remember the truth that you tend to forget.
It's easy to say "you only live once",
But for how many years,
Perhaps just a few months.

Ian Hughes, Wallasey, Merseyside

LIFE

What I love about my lovely life
Is to wake to to see my children and wife,
To walk about without a care,
To hear birds whistle in the sky, breathe in fresh air.

We all have worries and suffer pains,
But with all the losses, there's more gains,
We're all different, but that's the beauty of it
As long as you manage with life it's a hit.

People crave money and riches from God above,
But you just need enough to survive and lots of love.
We all feel down when we come into strife,
But we get through it because we all love life.

Some people are strong and some are weak,
Some are aggressive, some are very meek.
We have straight people, some sharp as a knife,
But we're all here for a reason, we've got a life.

P J Chadwick, St Helens, Merseyside

CHRISTMAS HEADLINES

More lights, more food, more booze,
Churches empty, pubs full.
Forget the poor and the homeless,
Book your Christmas meal now.
Meet Santa in his grotto,
It'll be two pounds, or five with a photo.

J Rapilliard, Liverpool, Merseyside

IF

If wishes were kisses
And tears were the sea
And hopes and desires
Grew strong as a tree
If moonbeams were my dreams
My lips to inspire
And yearning was burning
Like my heart on fire
If my thoughts and your thoughts
Could weave a new dawn
Of green hills and daffodils
And fields of gold corn
If my life and your life
Could sparkle as one
Of sharing and caring
As memories move on
If my love and your love
Could paint a blue sky
A rhapsody of rainbows
And never shall die

Bill Huddleston, Liverpool, Merseyside

MERCEDES FARMERS

Weeds stood against
A field fenced.
Barbed wire creeps
Slowly, rustling the metal
Jobs of farmers delight,
Loosely stealing the perfumed
Air of dung and doing,
Of earthy flight.
Yes, weeds stood against
A field fenced
And laughed at Mercedes farmers.

Derek Culley, Southport, Merseyside

THE PUNISHING WIND

The icy blue wind and the freezing gale,
Now cover the land and smother the frail.
This rapid mist that sweeps all around,
It will cover our land and freeze up the ground.

It snaps at the young and smiles at the old,
As it knows they are weak they're casualties of the cold.
Our walkways are covered with a blanket of ice,
It's a deadly trap and a nasty device.

But cold has no friends when it's acting this way,
As it leaves us isolated and trapped through the day.
It tightens its grip with a volley of hail,
With weapons like this it cannot fail.

When the land is quiet but for a whistling breeze,
Strewn all around lay broken-down trees.
It lifts up its cloak and then carries away,
All the innocent victims it's caught in that day.

David Brown, Liverpool, Merseyside